Build a BEAUTIFUL LIFE

out of BROKEN PIECES

Kris Reece

Build a Beautiful Life Out of Broken Pieces

Copyright © 2015 Kris Reece

ISBN: 978-0-9965172-0-1

Kris Reece
776 Mountain Blvd, Suite 106
Warren, NJ 07069
kris@krisreece.com
www.krisreece.com

Limits of Liability and Disclaimer of Warranty
The author and publisher shall not be liable for your misuse of this material. This book is strictly for informational and educational purposes.

Warning – Disclaimer
The purpose of this book is to educate and entertain. The author and/or publisher do not guarantee that anyone following these techniques, suggestions, tips, ideas, or strategies will become successful. The author and/or publisher shall have neither liability nor responsibility to anyone with respect to any loss or damage caused, or alleged to be caused, directly or indirectly by the information contained in this book.

Cover Art and Interior Design by Delaine Ulmer, StudioUltimateDesign.com

♥

This book is dedicated to every woman who wonders if I'm writing about her. You are more loved and have more potential than you can imagine, and more power at your disposal than you could ever need to fulfill your purpose.

CONTENTS

Acknowledgements **vii**

Foreword **ix**

Introduction **xiii**

17
CHAPTER 1
Where Do Broken Pieces Come From?

31
CHAPTER 2
What Hidden Beliefs Are Causing You to Suffer?

41
CHAPTER 3
Uncover Your Broken Pieces

55
CHAPTER 4
Tear Down the Walls

69
CHAPTER 5
Overcome Common Obstacles to Healing

85
CHAPTER 6
Is the Foundation Faulty?

93
CHAPTER 7
God Is the Master Builder

101
CHAPTER 8
The Building Blocks

109
CHAPTER 9
Nothing Is Wasted

115
CHAPTER 10
Keep Going During Inevitable Setbacks

121
CHAPTER 11
Are You Ready for Something Beautiful?

Appendix **129**

About the Author **148**

ACKNOWLEDGEMENTS

I would like to express my deepest gratitude to my husband, the love of my life. Without your support this book, and all that I do, would not be possible. Thank you for letting me be me.

I would like to thank my precious daughter, Zoe. You have inspired me to be a better woman. God has used you to shape me in more ways than you could even imagine. Thank you for growing with me.

Thank you to my coach, Dwight Bain. Your constant encouragement empowers me to soar. Thank you for your inspiration, education and motivation. Without your gentle suggestions, this book would have remained just an idea.

And thank you, Kate Hanley my writer and editor. Thank you for always staying on my timelines, for always being there for me and for softening my edges. This book truly came to life because of you.

FOREWORD

Everyone has pain of some kind. Sadly, many people hide it instead of heal from it. They let their pain become a part of their identity. They stay stuck in the brokenness of what could have been, instead of re-inventing themselves into who they are designed to be.

My friend, Kris Reece, was like that for too many years. She had a "perfect" life on the outside, but she was shattered and broken on the inside. Maybe you are like that. Maybe you try not to think about your painful past by staying busy; you're "productive" to avoid facing the sadness. Maybe you work hard to make your body, home, career or kids as flawless as possible so that nobody sees your pain—so that no one would ever guess you don't have your life together and are simply acting tough to get through the day.

Perhaps you have given up all hope that you could ever put the broken pieces together in any orderly way ever again. Maybe you feel like you are drowning in the pain of your past. Maybe you are living a nightmare instead of living your dreams, because you gave up trying to ever get better. You gave up on the hope of ever experiencing the happiness and fulfillment that come from having a healthy and restored life.

Too many people stay stuck in their fears or trapped in their addictions because they don't believe they can recover. They believe the lie that they are too far gone.

But broken lives can be repaired. In fact, in the hands of a master craftsman, they can be renovated to a much better and healthier place than before. Kris is one of those masters.

The book you are holding is a companion on your journey toward wholeness, toward being the person God designed you to be. You don't have to stay broken. You can heal, and this book will guide you, step by step, through that healing process.

Until you can believe that healing is possible, know that Kris will believe it for you. Her words and wisdom contained on these pages will walk you through the stages of deep healing and recovery toward becoming beautiful instead of staying broken. She has helped hundreds of people rebuild their broken dreams into beautiful lives, and she can help you, too.

Healing isn't easy, and building from brokenness is hard work. That's why there are dozens and dozens of powerful exercises included here, designed for you to work through and then hopefully share and process with your counselor, coach or small group. The more you heal and recover, the more it benefits you to share your story with others so they can also be encouraged to keep growing past their pain and brokenness.

This is your time to heal. This is your time to change. You have the right toolkit inside the pages of this book, and you have the right guide in Kris Reece. Now it's time to get started building from brokenness. Read on knowing your life is about to change—*forever.*

Dwight Bain
Strategic Change Expert
Orlando, FL

INTRODUCTION

I grew up with a tremendous amount of brokenness, which I carried with me into adult life. The funny thing is, I had no idea just how much hurt I was carrying around. I was so blind that I actually thought I had it all together and my stuff didn't stink!

It wasn't until my mid-30s that I realized my life was not all that I hoped it would be—that my attempts at love and gratification had left me feeling empty.

On the outside, it looked like I had the world at my feet: I ran a profitable business, had a beautiful daughter and was married to a successful financial advisor. Our home was large and beautifully decorated; in fact, it was once featured in a home-decorating magazine. The walls were lined with expensive artwork and trophies, and the garages held fancy cars and then some. I bought custom-made designer clothes. Money wasn't even an afterthought. I had everything I ever wanted…or so I thought.

The problem is, I was miserable. The successful business was a pleasant distraction to a loveless lie of a marriage. The McMansion was a facade for what should have been a happy family had it not been built on lies and deception. I felt so empty, so foolish. How did I end up here? I distracted myself as best I could with activities. But the only true joys I had in my life were my daughter and my growing relationship with Jesus.

It was a tough spot. When I slowed down from the busy distractions, I had to face the pain and the truth that I was not happy. If I kept going at the pace I had been, it was just going to be a short amount of time before I burned out again. I had a pivotal decision to make—continue to operate the same way while hoping for a different result, or face the discomfort head-on and pray I made it through to the other side.

I'm a confrontational person by nature, so you bet I took the "head-on" approach. Trying and failing was better than where I was. I was in a miserable marriage, I was in a career that I was good at but not passionate about and, worst of all, I felt as if I served no greater purpose in this world. Something had to change! And I knew the change had to begin in me.

I began the healing process by first owning that I was broken. I admit, I didn't acknowledge the full extent of my brokenness right away. It took years to do that—years of allowing myself to see my wounds and do the work to heal them. And through the process, I came to live a more joyful and abundant life than I could have ever imagined—a marriage to the love of my life, a new business that I'm absolutely passionate about, an inexplicable joy despite any circumstances. I have more now than money could ever purchase. That's not to say I don't have "stuff"—I have all the "stuff" I desire, and God keeps on blessing me, but it's the peace and joy that I appreciate the most. Years ago I would have paid any amount of money for that, and now I have it free of charge!

Every once in a while I am reminded of the way I felt prior to this healing, and I can't believe I'm the same person. Many women I counsel say the same thing about their journey from broken to beautiful. The things they struggle with would make you cry, mainly because you can probably relate. After spending years of feeling empty, frustrated and stuck with a sense of hopelessness, these women break through bonds toward a freedom they never expected.

Once they take the steps that I outline in this book, they are able to live a life of love, intimacy, greatly reduced anxiety and HOPE.

And on the other side, every single woman says to me, "The journey didn't take nearly as long as I thought."

That is what inspired me to write this book. Much of what I cover in these pages is the process I take each woman through that enables her to build something beautiful out of her broken pieces. Throughout the book, I share the true stories of my clients—as well as my own—so you can see real-world examples of how this work creates positive and powerful changes.

❤ HOW TO USE THIS BOOK

You can use this book in a variety of ways.

First, you can read it and work through the assignments on your own. It is, after all, a self-help book. Just make sure you stop and take the time to actually do the assignments I outline. I am not a busy-work kinda gal. I like to be productive, and I need whatever it is I'm doing to be done for good reason. These activities are for good reason: They are designed to bring you closer to who God intended you to be.

Second, you can walk this journey with a professional, whether it's a coach, a counselor or a therapist. Your broken pieces have been with you as long as they have because they are difficult to spot on your own—you have likely spent decades keeping them hidden, and they won't just automatically reveal themselves with 20/20 clarity. You don't have to do this alone!

Third, you can use this book in a group setting. Breaking each section down and spending ample time walking through the process with a few trusted friends or a support group will bring tremendous results.

No matter where you are on your journey, or how broken you feel, or how you decide to use this book, there is hope.

The only question you need to answer at this point is:

Are you ready to build something beautiful out of your broken pieces?

*"Brokenness is often
the road to breakthrough.
Be encouraged."*

~TONY EVANS

1

Where Do Broken
Pieces Come From?

Mary wakes up suddenly, like she does many mornings, to the frantic barking of dogs. This immediately raises her anxiety level to a 10. Mary thinks to herself, *I am so sick of these dogs. My husband asked for these dogs and promised to take care of them and train them. Where is he now? Doesn't he know that I am trying to sleep? I get so tired of him making empty promises just to get what he wants. I'm sick of being the one who has to be the bad guy all the time. He's the immature one. I'm tired of being taken advantage of. I can't talk to him anymore, he just yesses me. I don't even feel like looking at him this morning. All he thinks about is himself. He doesn't care about what I want or need.*

In her frustration, Mary heads downstairs to the kitchen and greets her husband with a half-hearted "G'mornin.'"

"What's wrong?" he asks.

"Nothing," Mary responds.

Jack pets the dogs, kisses her and heads out to work.

See, he doesn't care about how I feel.

She slams the door, gets ready for work and speeds off in her car, almost hitting the neighbor's cat. *What is it with these dumb animals,* she mutters to herself.

Mary begins her day determined that she has had enough from her husband and has to pursue a divorce, there is just no other option. He is immature and unreliable.

Mary is unaware that her default thoughts were created by something that was broken in her past. It could be the distant past or the recent past, but those experiences created a core belief (which we will talk more about in Chapter 2).

Once Mary and I sat down and talked through these thoughts and the feelings that accompanied them, we found that her husband wasn't such an immature and unreliable man. Rather, he often did more than she expected in terms of meeting her needs. We also discovered that Mary's father and first husband expected everything to be perfect, and she was criticized when they weren't. Mary knows that perfection isn't possible, yet she still strives for it. And since it's not possible, she always falls short.

The real eye opener for Mary was realizing that she became angry and defensive BEFORE anyone could criticize her. This was a protective mechanism that may have served a purpose in the past, but it had the potential to destroy her current marriage if she didn't learn to change her reactions.

Many of us suffer from having responses that were appropriate and perhaps even necessary for survival at one point in our lives, but are no longer serving a good purpose. In fact, they are slowly killing our relationships, because we are relating to others from a place of brokenness, not health and wholeness.

♥ THE SURPRISING ORIGIN OF BROKEN PIECES

There are some people who can easily pinpoint a specific event that wounded them greatly. It may have been years in the past, but every time they think about it or talk about it—or they experience anything that even mildly resembles that old situation—it triggers the same emotional reaction as when it first happened. This is a deep wound that needs deep healing.

But there are also many of us who do not have one obvious traumatic event. Rather, we have dozens of little emotional wounds that never healed properly, leaving us with the same need for deep healing.

You see, wounds are like roots. They each go deep. And whether big or small, they each have a purpose: Where roots provide stability and sustenance, wounds all too often create instability and a lack of access to the things that nourish us—things like love, faith and trust.

> WOUNDS CREATE INSTABILITY AND A LACK OF ACCESS TO THE THINGS THAT NOURISH US—THINGS LIKE LOVE, FAITH AND TRUST.

When you experience a scarring event, that wound takes root and contributes to your core beliefs—fundamental

19

concepts that live beneath your level of consciousness that shape your perceptions of reality, and sometimes shape reality itself. So when you experience a new challenging event, you don't try to create a new response to protect yourself—you draw on your core beliefs to dictate how to respond. And these responses are typically overreactions.

Think of a time when you had an outsize reaction to something—maybe it was an inexplicable sadness, a lashing out, or a complete withdrawal inside a wall of protection. At the root of that response was a core belief.

❤ EXPLORING YOUR "ROOTS"

Some of you may be reading this and saying, "I don't think I'm broken, it's the other people in my life who have the problem." I encourage you to please keep reading. Even if someone else is the problem, your response is your responsibility.

Many of you reading this are saying, "Kris, I know I'm broken; I just don't even know where to begin to untangle the mess and figure it out. It all seems so overwhelming that I want to give up before I even start." Trust me when I say that there is no such thing as being beyond repair. Perhaps my own story will inspire you:

My brokenness began long before I could remember, when my parent's marriage failed before I was two. My grandmother explained my father's absence by saying that he was not a good man and that he was hardly ever home. I never knew my biological father except for two short visits inside of 20 years.

I was torn: On one hand, I would have liked to know my father (since passed), but my fear of upsetting my mother and step-father kept me from admitting those feelings, even to myself. On the other hand, I felt rejected. Why hadn't he tried harder to see me, sent me birthday cards, something?? I could hear my mother and grandmother say what a jerk he was, but my heart longed to be loved and accepted.

By the age of two, I had a stepfather who had some issues of his own, which kept him from being able to pay me much attention. I just wanted to be loved, but everywhere I turned it was unavailable.

Then along came my new baby sister. What little attention that had been available was now given to her. I hated her. I felt so lonely and so sad, and I wasn't even five years old yet.

Next, my life went blank for about seven years. I truly don't remember much, other than a constant supply of anger and criticism, intermingled with a few encouraging comments that only confused me further. Was I a good girl or not? Was I worthy of love or not?

Being acknowledged one day and punished the next created so much confusion in me that I wanted to die. My heart cried, *Someone please notice me—I am a good girl! I want your love!! Please see me!!* And I cried, too. All the time. I soothed myself by crying until I fell sleep. I would get sufficiently exhausted and finally be able to drift off into "I don't have to think about my life" land.

When I was in my early teens, I learned that my stepfather struggled with mental disorders and that my mother was so consumed by his needs, she had little to nothing left to give us kids. My older brother, younger sister and I were not close at all. We were all in protective mode, so although we lived in the same house, I can honestly say that I remember very little about our lives together.

By my teen years, I had long given up on getting love from my family. So I opened myself up to relationships with boys. I did have girls as friends, but I needed to get noticed and my girlfriends couldn't fill that need. But teenage boys certainly could!

I had my first boyfriend at age 14. I gave myself over to this boy in ways that I wish I hadn't, but he was the first person who ever made me feel special. He gave me all of his attention and I LOVED IT! I needed it! My heart breaks when I remember how I broke off our relationship on the first day of freshman year of high school. I did it because someone else was paying attention to me and I had the thrill of being noticed again. I had come to crave that attention and I pursued it. It wasn't hard to find—I was an attractive young girl screaming "look at me."

After that first sweet relationship that I heartlessly ended, I had two boyfriends who each dumped me. The rejection I felt was horrific—not a good development for a needy young girl looking for true love. I had nowhere to turn, no one to help me. I knew I deserved better, I just didn't know how to get it.

One thing I did know was that being sweet wasn't working. So I emerged a cold, bitter, defensive young lady with walls no one could penetrate. I ran as far away from God as possible and right into the arms of any dysfunctional relationship I could find. This time, the only difference was the tough girl mask I wore and the fortress of sarcasm I hid inside to help ensure I was never going to get hurt again.

One relationship after another, I began to chew men up and spit them out. No one was going to hurt me—that was my motto. And I proceeded to live life this way for quite some time.

This story actually gets worse from here, but before I go any further, I want to stop and issue you a challenge: Go back and reread my story, but this time with the goal of counting the number of wounds that were created and never healed.

If you're unsure—or if you lost count—I'll tell you the answer: By the age of 22, I had developed at least 10 deep wounds that affected how I felt about myself and how I related to others by contributing to my core beliefs.

❤ WHAT ARE YOUR WOUNDS?

We all have a story to tell. And each of our stories can be broken down into large or small injuries that have left cracks, or what I call brokenness.

I know you've heard the phrase, "If it ain't broke, don't fix it." Odds are, that's how you've approached life, not realizing that those cracks in your foundation are contributing to tremendous emotional instability. Those cracks explain why one woman will go ballistic if her husband doesn't call her, while another will remain unfazed. Or why one woman can take constructive criticism in stride while another finds herself getting angry or running in the bathroom to cry.

It's tempting to view these reactions as personality traits, and while sometimes they are a part of our genetic makeup, more often they are a result of brokenness in us. And when pressure is put on a broken place, it creates great stress as its instability is unable to handle pressure.

There are many different circumstances that can create brokenness inside of us. Below is just a partial list of them. These are based on the work of Tim Clinton and Gary Sibcy, particularly in their book, *Why You Do the Things You Do:*

Minor Injury/Short Duration

- Parent shows up late to pick up child
- Parent is upset, tense, stressed
- Parent has flu and is temporarily unavailable to the child
- Adult often shows up late for work or appointments
- Spouse goes out of town for a week

Do you relate to any of these? Stephanie did. She came to me unsure why she always felt anxious and angry when her husband was late. She described Jack as a wonderful, loving husband who would do anything for her, but his lateness drove her crazy. She was threatening divorce to get him to change.

When we delved deeper into Stephanie's past she revealed that her mother was always extremely punctual, and made Stephanie feel as if she were failing miserably if she wasn't on time. Stephanie worked hard to show her mother that she could be a good girl and be on time. But now her husband, the man who was supposed to love her, was doing such an egregious, unloving act.

When Stephanie was able to apply her reaction to her current relationship and not the one imposed on her by her mother, the hurt and the intensity subsided.

Even though having a punctual mother is relatively minor on the brokenness scale, it still has the power to affect your relationships adversely.

Minor Injury/Long Duration

- Caregiver is constantly unavailable
- Parent is never there for the big things: first baseball game, school play, karate practice, dance lessons, etc.
- Parents divorce amicably without post-divorce conflict
- Spouse works too much in order to avoid home life
- Adult is emotionally distant
- Adult demonstrates ongoing insensitivity
- Spouse in uninvolved in family life

Jackson found himself in this category when, for the life of him, he couldn't figure out why he was so clingy in his relationships. They would all start out great, but eventually his dating partner would end the relationship. He felt tremendous rejection.

Jackson's family was intact. Dad worked hard to provide and was a good man. Mom worked part time and volunteered at the church. Jackson's parents would be considered "good" parents, except for their emotional unavailability.

It took Jackson quite some time to realize that, despite the fact that his parents weren't "bad people," everything in his home was superficial. A lot of, "Oh that's nice dear." Jackson didn't realize that he spent his childhood hoping for the love and attention he craved but rarely ever received. So when he entered into his own relationships, these women were so willing to listen to him and love him that he couldn't get enough. Ultimately, his subconscious need for large amounts of attention would lead to the end of the relationship—the very thing he feared the most.

Severe Injury/Short Duration

- Parent goes to hospital for a week
- Child is sick and parent is unavailable
- Child gets lost for brief period of time
- Spouse has an extramarital affair
- Adults engage in intense arguments and verbal abuse
- Physical or sexual abuse occurs more than one or two times
- Complicated grief after loss of parent(s)

Many would call Linda one of the hardest-working women they have ever met. She works hard, she plays hard and she doesn't quit. She is the primary breadwinner for her home. As a high-level executive for a marketing firm, her job is non-stop. Linda came to me because she just didn't feel happy. "I have it all," she said, and by this world's standards, she did: sports cars, trips around the world, beautiful homes. Why then was she always so sad?

We reached back into Linda's upbringing. It wasn't a happy one—certainly not one where a child felt free to be herself. No, Linda was the caregiver in the home. Her mother suffered from mental breaks and was frequently hospitalized. Linda knew she could never count on her mother to be available for her or her siblings, so Linda had to step up. She not only cared for her younger brothers but often had to care for her mother as well.

After having worked with Linda for several months, she came to realize that she felt she had to be in constant control or life would fall apart.

It took some undoing, but Linda now lives and practices letting others take care of themselves, and she even lets them make their own mistakes. "It's liberating," she says.

Severe Injury/Long Duration

- Parents have an abusive marriage
- Parents divorce with ongoing conflict post-divorce
- Sibling gets chronic illness such as diabetes, stealing parent's time and attention
- Spouse gets involved in frequent extra-marital affairs
- Domestic violence—by parent or spouse—is chronic
- Addictive behavior—of parent or spouse—is chronic
- Family is dealing with long-term, life-threatening illness

Allison's parents divorced when she was seven. She remembers a happy life. In fact, for the longest time, she dreamed of her parents getting back together. Despite the fact that her mother had several extramarital affairs and that her father slept in another room, Allison remembers life being perfect. If her parents would just say "I love you," she thought, they could get back together and forget all about the bad stuff.

This thought process may be endearing as a seven-year-old, but when it's a 16-year-old whose wounds damaged her so greatly that she remains stuck in a seven-year-old mindset, it becomes more problematic.

But it doesn't end there. Allison has carried this flair for fantasy into other areas of her life. Instead of participating in reality, she prefers to get absorbed in books and her imagination. Many would misinterpret this young lady to be smart and studious, but tragically her introversion has become a protection, a way of hiding from reality.

I am so thankful when I get the opportunity to work with young ladies, because it is so much easier to heal wounds and re-write thought patterns that have just taken root. As an adult, if you don't heal from your wounds, you tend to just find more innovative ways to hide them, justify them or flat out ignore them.

There are many other examples of early wounds too numerous to list, including bullying, rejection by the opposite sex, being overweight, etc. When you brush any of these events aside and don't deal with the emotions, you are left with un-healed injuries. When something happens later in life that bears any resemblance to these earlier events, it's like getting slapped on an open wound. It hurts and your reactions are severe.

Your Assignment
IDENTIFY YOUR WOUNDS

It's time to start the healing process. And the first step is to begin examining your wounds.

Find a quiet spot where you will not be interrupted. Write down the wounds from your past. Some will come to mind right away, others will take quiet reflection. This is not a time to judge or evaluate whether or not you think it should be no big deal. If it hurt you back then, write it down—no matter how silly it seems now.

After you have written the ones that come to mind immediately, take a few minutes of quiet time with God and ask Him to reveal any others you have been suppressing. As you quietly sit before God, remember not to expect Him to speak in an audible voice. He often speaks to us with impressions on our heart and soul, or with pictures in our mind. Don't dismiss anything that comes to mind. Capture it all. Trust me, God wants to see you healed, and He will equip you with everything necessary to get you there. By taking this step, you're on your way!

NOTES

---

*"We are products of
our past, but we don't
have to be prisoners to it."*

~RICK WARREN

2
What Hidden Beliefs
Are Causing You to Suffer?

My story of longing to be seen and loved is pretty common. But it pales in comparison to the deep wounds that some souls have endured—perhaps even yours. No matter how deep or traumatic, one thing that is true of wounds of all sizes is that they are typically not easy to see—especially to those who bear them. Some of the wounded—including me—go so far as to put a big smile on and pretend nothing is wrong. *Nothing to see here, folks, I'm fine.* If you tell yourself a lie long enough, you'll start to believe it.

I certainly started to believe that I was fine. Those wounds damaged some of the deepest parts of my soul, leaving them screaming for healing. On the surface, though, I looked like I had it all together. I even thought I had it all together! And yet, in every relationship I had, the issues I tried so hard to bury always showed up.

When you experience a deep soul wound, your subconscious mind tries to make sense of it—to come up with a rule or code of behavior that will protect you from another similar experience. These thoughts solidify into a core belief, which then becomes deeply imbedded in your psyche. Any time you experience stress, those core beliefs will emerge again and again. This means big-ticket items such as divorce, death and abuse, etc. It also means everyday instances—an interaction with your spouse, for example, that triggers those old wounds and causes you to react in an outsized way.

Here is an example of what I mean: Samantha's parents divorced when she was young. Her mother was trying to manage her own emotions while creating a new life and new relationships. Meaning, she didn't have a lot of capacity to deal with Samantha's needs. And Samantha's temperament required constant attention and reassurance, which her mother was too busy and too tired to give. (Refer to the appendix for more on temperament.) This was Samantha's first deep wound.

Samantha's father was in her life and showed her a tremendous amount of love, but little in the way of discipline. There was very little structure in his home, and she knew she could get away with anything. This caused confusion for Samantha—another wound.

As she got older and her mother's life stabilized and healed, Samantha was able to draw closer to her and get some of her emotional needs met. But by that point Samantha was hesitant and confused. She knew that her mother was always there for her, but due to her father's spoiling and lack of discipline, Samantha assumed that life went how she demanded it would go.

When her mother tried to discipline Samantha, it didn't go over well. Samantha would react in ways that caused a tremendous amount of tension for all involved. There was a time where Samantha's mother had given her a gift card for her birthday. Samantha lost this gift card and told her mother that she needed a new one, but her mother didn't replace it. Samantha saw this as a punishment and got very upset. Samantha's mother tried to explain that it would cost money to replace it. Many parents right now reading this will agree with Samantha's mother's attempt to use this opportunity to teach responsibility. But since it was her father's style to just buy another one, it led Samantha to believe that her mother was being harsh and punishing.

Samantha had developed a core belief that love meant a lack of discipline. So whenever her mother tried to enforce a point, Samantha thought it meant she was bad and unlovable, which caused her to lash out in anger. Everything became an argument.

Most parents would have assumed that this was a "normal" phase that tweens go through. But Samantha's mother knew enough to see that Samantha was a wounded little girl in need of healing before her reactions grew into something out of control.

By this point, Samantha's father had remarried. While the first few years with the step-mother were wonderful, things shifted over time. The step-mother had gone from loving Samantha like her own to wanting her own child. The comments she made left Samantha feeling confused and hurt. This caused the next deep wound: Samantha's confusion grew and she became fearful of giving or asking for love from this woman.

In the years to come, Samantha felt more and more rejected by her father and step-mother—her father took the step-mother's side, commanding Samantha to put a smile on her face and get over it. He yelled at her anytime she wasn't smiling.

Samantha didn't come to realize until years later that her step-mother was hurt and angry that Samantha had come to have a great relationship with her mother. You see, the step-mother had wanted to be the primary mother figure in Samantha's life. And so she spent several years making sarcastic, belittling comments about both Samantha and her mother.

By this point, Samantha had no idea who to trust. And it deepened one of her initial wounds: confusion.

Although Samantha knew the Lord and had a very strong personality, she struggled with a fear of rejection. This fear caused her to keep to herself. She kept both her feelings and her hopes inside, as she was never quite sure what she would get met with.

She also had a deep sense of distrust. Now that she is an adult with a primary relationship of her own, she jumps to wrong conclusions on many occasions because she doesn't know how to trust. This even spills over into her relationship with God: She is scared to trust Him, despite how much she wants to.

In Samantha's story, you can see the traumatic effects that everyday events can have on the soul. My clients are always surprised at how such little things can make a big impact on how we relate to others. And when left untreated, they grow into something uncontrollable and deadly. Before we move on to the healing process, let's delve a little further into some examples of core beliefs and how they manifest.

❤ HOW EARLY WOUNDS SHOW UP IN YOUR LIFE

As you can see in the stories I've shared, including my own, emotional wounds create core beliefs and those core beliefs shape our perceptions of reality, our reactions and our relationships.

To simplify, I would like to break things down for you into bite-size chunks. There are three basic categories of core beliefs and three unhealthy ways a person responds to these beliefs.

The three basic categories of core beliefs are:

- **Conformity:** This belief causes people to seek approval in order to attain love. This belief requires approval from everyone and leads to a fear that if the person is truly known, she will be rejected. This is not always the case, but depressed clients often have conforming beliefs.

- **Compulsivity:** These beliefs are rooted in the assumption that one is loved based on performance. This belief says that you should be competent and earn people's love through accomplishments. This is not always the case, but anxious and eating-disordered clients often have compulsive beliefs.

- **Control:** These beliefs relate to control of oneself and/ or others. This belief says that if you are not in control of yourself or others, something must be done, as a lack of control is not to be tolerated. This is not always the case, but angry clients often have controlling beliefs.

On the surface, all of these beliefs on the surface can appear to be strengths, or even your best qualities. All the more reason why you need to tear down the walls to see what is buried underneath.

The three unhealthy ways a person typically responds to soul wounds are:

1. **Protective.** Let's say your parents fought constantly when you were little, and perhaps even divorced. Or you may have suffered sexual or emotional abuse at the hands of those who should have loved you. Perhaps you had the picture-perfect family on the outside but felt unloved. You may have coped by disconnecting emotionally from other people. If you learned to survive your wounds by protecting yourself, you likely:

   • Don't like to share your feelings with others
   • Have a hard time understanding how other people feel
   • Deal with stressful situations by yourself
   • Value your independence
   • Don't care about being accepted or rejected by others—either because you truly aren't fazed by others' opinions of you, or because your fear of rejection prompts you to reject others first
   • Value personal achievements over relationships

Beliefs that fuel protection stem from trust. You feel that you are worthy of love based upon your accomplishments. You feel that you need to depend on your own abilities and yourself. You believe that others are either unwilling or incapable of loving you. But the biggest part is that you feel that others cannot be trusted. You may also have an inflated sense of self and think less of others. You most likely turn away from God and other people and look to yourself for comfort. You are often angry and resentful toward God. The most full-blown cases can be narcissistic, self-sufficient or compulsively perfectionistic.

2. **Needy.** People who respond to wounds from an emotional place tend to cling, and vary widely in their moods and feelings. If you fit this profile, you:

- Share more about your feelings than your partner
- Have feelings (such as anger, sadness or anxiety) that get out of control quickly
- Worry A LOT about being alone and being abandoned
- Tend to want to be closer to others than others do in return
- Desperately seek comfort and support during a stressful time

The core belief at the root here is that you are not worthy of love. Somewhere along the way, you learned that you cannot get the love you need without being angry, clingy or desperate. You likely have a tremendous fear of abandonment and rejection. You probably go from one relationship to the next, perhaps even hiding relationships for a while to make it seem to others as if you had been waiting to find the right person.

The effects of this response are a low self-confidence and a fear of making decisions. You are perpetually seeking advice—on the phone with one friend to the next saying the same thing to each person. It may feel like you can't live without others, and you are likely to depend on others far more than they depend on you.

3. **Protective and needy.** Yet another way of handling yourself is a combination of the two, which causes confusion for both you and the people around you. These are some typical responses of the protective and needy type:

- You tend to avoid feelings all together
- Your feelings are very intense and overwhelming
- You want to be close to people but push them away at the same time
- You can be clingy one moment and distant and aloof another
- You want to let people in but fear rejection
- You feel very vulnerable in relationships
- You can't decide whether you truly want to be in close relationships

As you might guess by reading the above list—and perhaps may recognize from your own life—this coping mechanism is confusing, because people will never know where they stand with you, and you may not know yourself how you truly feel about others. That's because you struggle with feeling like everything is dark and that you are not lovable or worthy of love.

If you are in an abusive relationship, you probably feel that you deserve it. This type of response typically comes from a very traumatic (abusive) past. The scary part of this response is that the trauma from the past is buried very deep, so these people tend to be functioning quite well on the surface, but they have a weak sense of identity.

Your Assignment
SEARCH FOR YOUR CORE BELIEFS

To begin to uncover some of the beliefs that have shaped you...

Identify your recurring thoughts. Start by circling all of the ways that you respond in the examples above. What kinds of core beliefs do the responses you circled suggest? Remember, core beliefs run deep, and they like to hide. Rarely do people walk around with the conscious awareness that they will reject people first before they get rejected, or that they are unable to submit to authority because they vowed never to be taken advantage of. But these are prime examples of core beliefs. What are yours?

List your common overreactions. If you don't know what they are, the people closest to you will. Ask for their help in helping you improve. Ask them, "What do you feel I commonly overreact to?" and "Under which circumstances do my responses seem out of character or place?"

If you are having a hard time with this exercise, it's no surprise: Your ego has been working very hard for a very long time to keep these core beliefs hidden from your sight. The process of seeing these hidden beliefs can be difficult without the objective help of a professional. You can't see what you can't see. Keep in mind, I am always a resource for you—I may be able to help you myself or refer you to someone who can.

NOTES

_____

_____

_____

_____

_____

_____

_____

_____

_____

_____

_____

_____

_____

_____

_____

_____

_____

_____

_____

*"I use the bits and pieces
of others' personalities
to form my own."*

~KURT COBAIN

3

Uncover Your Broken Pieces

As a young girl, Gigi had a dream, one that included a handsome husband, two children, a dog and a white picket fence. This dream had no basis in real life—Gigi's childhood was anything but storybook—but it was powerful.

Gigi was dead-set on making this dream come true by the time she was 20. She tried with every boy she dated. Some were scared off, while others saw the opportunity to play into her fantasy to get what they wanted.

So it happened with Brad. Brad came from a good family. He was attractive, and his family owned their own business. Yet there were some things about Brad that didn't sit right with Gigi. For instance, he would check out other girls as they walked by. And sometimes Brad wouldn't call her for days. Gigi didn't want to call him out on these behaviors because everything else was so great. Besides, all guys do that, she thought. And he was everything she had ever hoped for.

Gigi had wanted to save herself for marriage, but with Brad that no longer mattered. She had found her man. Everything was going to be perfect.

But Gigi quickly learned the truth when she became pregnant at 21. Her heart was broken when Brad threatened to leave her if she didn't have an abortion. "This is going to completely mess up my plans," he said.

"Your plans?" Gigi replied.

"Oh you know what I meant, I meant our plans. How do you think we are ever going to manage a child at our age? If we wait to have a family then it will be perfect."

Gigi bought into his reasoning and desperately wanted to keep Brad and her dream, so she proceeded with the abortion.

Gigi was not prepared for the emotions that followed. *Did I just give up my dream? No, I can't think like that, I have to move forward. My life is going to be great. I will do whatever I need to do to forget about this. My future is too bright.*

It wasn't long before Brad dumped Gigi for another girl. This sent Gigi into a tailspin of emotions. But she was not about to alter her dream, so instead she altered her feelings.

Afraid of loving at that level again, Gigi took the route of hiding, disguising and burying her true feelings and desires in an effort to hold onto the dream. She later married a man she didn't love because she wanted the security he brought.

It took 23 more years of being unhappy and unfulfilled before Gigi took action to come in for healing from the deep issues hiding behind the lies.

❤ WHY WE HIDE OUR BROKEN PIECES IN THE FIRST PLACE

The longing in everyone's heart—including yours, I'm sure of it—is to be loved, and loved unconditionally for who they truly are. If you have ever experienced unconditional love, you know the joy that comes from simply being yourself, quirks, warts and all.

If we are all in search of this type of love, why then do we spend so much time and energy on hiding our brokenness? If you are like most of the women I meet in my practice, you dress up your scars, slap on a smile, and try to mold yourself into what you think a person who is worthy of unconditional love should look like rather than pursue true healing. I know; I did a lot of pretending in the past, too.

Because my father rejected me as a little girl, I adopted a tough-girl attitude as an adult. I used men for sex and vowed that I would never be hurt again. I actually believed I was happy and that my way was working for me. I also thought that any woman who devoted her life to a man was a fool. I guess that's why they call it self-deception, because, of course, what I longed for more than anything else was to be in a loving relationship with a man.

So why do we focus on hiding instead of healing? We hide our broken pieces for three reasons:

We fear vulnerability. To admit you need healing is to allow yourself to be vulnerable. And vulnerability is practically a dirty word in our culture. Woman are so afraid of vulnerability they avoid it all costs—it's not just a male trait. In an age where 1,000 Facebook friends is the norm and "We must get together for lunch" is recited at the end of every meet-up, you may feel like you lack what it takes to build the true, deep relationships that can make you feel loved.

I BELIEVE EVERYONE HAS WHAT IT TAKES TO HEAL FROM BROKENNESS, BUT LIKE MANY DIFFICULT THINGS IN LIFE, IT SEEMS EASIER TO TAKE A SHORTCUT.

But are you truly lacking, or is your ability just in need of a little strengthening?

What you don't realize is that you have to expend tremendous energy on pretending your wounds don't exist. Perhaps you took your brokenness to school to get an education that will hopefully disguise it. Or brushed it under the rug in hopes that no one will trip over it. Or decided to ignore it by having babies and believing they are the answer to your desire for love. Or perhaps you recite positive statements to yourself and go through your day with a big, phony smile on your face pretending you are happy, but behind closed doors it's a different story.

The reason behind all of these interchangeable masks is fear. *If someone truly saw who I was and what I've been through, there is no possible way they would like me.*

The vulnerability I am talking about is not the victim mentality that happily relates its woes onto everyone. It is not emotionally vomiting on people when they ask you simply, "How are you?"

No, the vulnerability I'm referring to is one that allows the cracks to show. When you shine light on the cracks, the light shows through. *That's* what you want people to see when they look at you. NO ONE is perfect. Please stop trying to pretend that you are. Each of us is flawed and broken, but God's strength is made perfect in our weakness (2 Corinthians 12:9). When you put aside your fear of being vulnerable, His light is able to shine through. When His radiant, beautiful light shines through, what do you think people see: the crack or the amazing light? That's right, they aren't focused on your cracks, they only see Jesus. And what a wonderful sight to see.

So I urge you, use the cover-up for your uneven skin tone, but stop trying to cover up the brokenness. You are stopping His light from shining through.

We have false expectations. False expectations come in two forms: ones you put on yourself and ones you allow others to put on you.

You know false expectations are at play when you hear yourself saying or thinking the words "should" and "ought" a lot. These ideas about what the "right'" thing to do could be coming from your expectations or from someone else's, but either way, there is always a voice that makes you feel as if you are missing the mark. So instead of facing these demons head-on, you pretend that it's OK. Or, you find a happy medium. Singing as a hobby is not a happy medium when you know you could do so much more with your gift. Painting as a hobby because you ought to have a steady, full-time job is no consolation, except if you have convinced yourself that the oughts and shoulds are somehow more true that your inborn talents and desires.

Oughts and shoulds get intermingled with God's true purpose for our lives, and the waters get muddied. Yes, there are things we should do in life. For example, we should be kind to others, we should brush our teeth in the morning and we should eat well-balanced meals. But when your shoulds are conceived in your own mind— and not from an objective, non-judgmental source—it gets confusing.

Take, for example, the woman who says she should pack her children's lunch, make a home-cooked dinner and keep the house perfectly clean each day. These are self-imposed shoulds. When your shoulds leave you in distress and let others take advantage of you, this is where the waters get murky.

Perhaps you are the workaholic who feels she should always be available for her clients. This sounds admirable in theory, but what about your family who feels left out of your life? Or maybe you are the woman who shoulds all over other people, like your husband. You say, "He should know what I am going through and just step up. He should just get off my case and leave me alone." These are shoulds that you imposed yourself and that aren't contributing joy and health to your life.

The same applies to oughts. To say, "I ought to work another day each week to catch up on my bills" when you are already working six days a week is not healthy. To say, "I ought to spend time with God to show Him I trust Him" is the beginning of a healthy ought, so long as it leads to action.

Oughts and shoulds can either lead you to change poor behavior or cause you to set unrealistic expectations of yourself and others. And when you have unrealistic expectations, there is one thing that always occurs: disappointment.

We feel there is no hope. You may have gone so far as to convince yourself that your wounds have happened for a reason, perhaps by repeating sayings such as, "What hasn't killed me, has made me stronger" and, "Oh, that was so long ago, I just put it out of my mind."

Whether you consciously or unconsciously decided that there was nothing you could do to prevent or to heal from the wounds, you lost your hope for recovery all the same.

This reason breaks my heart the most, because when a woman has given up on herself and her dreams, it is difficult to work through. If this is you, please don't give up hope. Rekindle the dreams you have in your heart. There is love waiting for you. Your dreams are waiting for you. Only you can fulfill them.

Reach out and get help—the kind of help that will walk you through the trauma and then through the healing. There is too much freedom and love waiting at the end of the road for you to remain broken. There is too much happiness and joy. This is not only a promise of mine, this is a promise to you from Almighty God. Read it for yourself: "Weeping may endure for a night, but joy cometh in the morning." (Psalm 30:5)

If this is you and you admit to yourself that you need help, begin your search for a Christian counselor—you need to work with someone who can point you to the One with all the answers. The One who holds each tomorrow. If you have been through sexual abuse, find a counselor who specializes in healing such trauma.

If you reach a dead-end, please don't hesitate to contact my team and I through *krisreece.com*. My practice specializes in helping women heal their brokenness and become all they were created to be. We will do all we can to connect you with someone in your area who can help.

❤ HOW CAN I START TO UNCOVER MY BROKEN PIECES?

I'll tell you this: Broken pieces almost always show up as inappropriate reactions.

Have you ever wondered how in the world your conversation with your significant other spiraled into an all-out argument that made both of you wonder why you ever got married in the first place?

I have. And I know you have, too. We've all been there.

And for the vast majority, it feels impossible to figure out why it happened. If you're the analytical type, you probably wish you had a tape recorder to rewind to see where it all went wrong. Your hunch is that it was something he said, or how he incorrectly perceived what you said that ignited this fire.

If you're more emotional, you tend to get overwhelmed by the whole affair. You end the argument with a kiss or the silent treatment for a week, and you avoid any urges to go back and review what happened and why it all went south. There is no true conflict resolution, merely the hope that time will pass and you will "feel" like reconnecting. The problem with this approach is that it doesn't help you two the next time old wounds get triggered. And trust me, there is always a next time.

It can be very difficult to be able to clearly see how your old wounds continue to influence your behavior. Some people may be quick to admit that they do have old wounds, while others are oblivious. But even those who admit they are broken can't put their finger on how those broken pieces are showing up in their life. Some are able to describe generally what they're struggling with, but they typically explain those struggles away by blaming someone or something else.

You can see why it's virtually impossible for someone to begin the repair process if they don't know where their problems live. It's like a plumber coming in to fix a leaky pipe with no knowledge of plumbing and NO idea where the problem originates.

Here are some typical original wounds and the way they often show up in later years:

Abandonment. If your biological father (or any significant authority figure) was absent in your early life, as an adult you are likely to enter into relationships with walls of protection. These walls create a defensiveness and argumentativeness that you just don't see. Your marriage is likely to break up, leaving you with more wounds from rejection and distrust. This only further solidifies your need for defense. If no healing takes place, it will only lead to poor choices and more brokenness.

Criticism. If you grew up in a home where perfection or performance determined whether or not you were considered good or bad, you are likely to develop a critical spirit, which then keeps you feeling separate from the people you love. This could have come from a perfectionistic parent or from a parent who struggled with her own insecurities and found it easy to point her dissatisfaction about herself onto you.

As much as this may have hurt growing up, whether the criticism came in an overt or a covert fashion, you are likely to develop the same method of criticizing—by picking on every little thing. Your relationships with men turn into love-hate relationships. And although you portray a haughty attitude, you are left hating yourself. Healing needs to take place to be delivered from this critical spirit, so you can respond to people with love.

Defensiveness. You can be defensive in two ways: in an attacking, cutthroat manner or, more subtly, by playing the victim. Children who grew up in a defensive home tend to adopt this from parents who aren't gentle in the way they communicate, perhaps as an effect of substance abuse.

If you are defensive, you typically had a parent whose wounds have not been healed. Perhaps you were attacked verbally simply because you wanted to go out to the movies with friends. You will have felt that you needed to defend yourself, and not just this one time, but over and over again to the point of it becoming a habitual form of communication. Now as an adult, any form of questioning evokes a level of defensiveness in you that seems extreme for the situation. It places an exhausting strain on your relationships.

Manipulation. This is one of the least detectable broken pieces. Many people who were manipulated as children don't realize it until years later, and when they do see it, their feelings can range from anger to resentment. If you grew up in a home where you were made to feel guilty for your opinions, likes and desires, especially if they went against your parents' beliefs, you are likely the target of manipulation. You were not allowed to think for yourself, and found yourself only receiving acceptance when you were doing what your parent or parents desired.

I see this often in cases of divorce, where one parent makes a child feel guilty for wanting to spend time with their other parent. In many cases, this parent manipulates circumstances to their benefit and lies to cover up their actions. It bears repeating: Manipulative behavior can go undetected for years before children eventually figure it out.

Personally, I find this one of the worst forms of abuse, as it is inflicted on a continual basis with no regard for the devastation it is causing the child. The motive is always purely selfish. And when the goal is not attained, there is hell to pay. Unfortunately, if you grew up in a manipulative environment, you probably don't know another way of getting what you want, so you resort to the same behavior. As an adult, you do the manipulating in an effort to have someone else take care of you, because you suspect that if you ask for support outright, you will be denied. So you resort to deception and orchestrating to get others to do your bidding. And if others don't go along, you likely subconsciously turn to a different tactic: either crocodile tears to elicit sympathy or yelling as a form of intimidation.

If you learned to manipulate others to get what you want, you likely have a deep-rooted fear that others will reject you. If this is you, I promise you that you are loved just the way you are. Manipulation tactics aren't necessary. In fact, if you keep using them, you'll only drive people away.

Every one of these broken pieces translates into how you relate to our Heavenly Father. If you experienced criticism, you are likely to believe that God is not pleased with you. If you had a fractured relationship with your father, you likely struggle with trusting our Heavenly Father. If you learned to be defensive, you probably either have built walls to keep Him out, or fear you're too damaged to be loved by Him. If you were manipulated, you probably feel you can't trust Him. And if you are the manipulator, you probably try to bargain with God without truly submitting to His will.

Your Assignment
UNCOVER YOUR BROKEN PIECES

To get a clearer look at your broken pieces, ask yourself these questions:

☐ YES   ☐ NO   Do I pretend that I am happy when I actually feel sad/angry/depressed?

☐ YES ☐ NO Are there areas of my life that I hope NO ONE ever finds out about?

☐ YES ☐ NO Do I have strong feelings rise up when I think about a particular time of my life or a specific person?

☐ YES ☐ NO Am I frequently exhausted?

☐ YES ☐ NO Do I tend to over-think things?

☐ YES ☐ NO Do I say yes when I would rather say no?

☐ YES ☐ NO Do I find dreams to be unrealistic and unattainable? Perhaps silly?

☐ YES ☐ NO Am I the one who says, "I'm not negative, I'm a realist"?

☐ YES ☐ NO Do I have only two speeds: warp or crash?

☐ YES ☐ NO Upon reflection, I wonder if my life would be different if _____ (can you ponder the IF)?

☐ YES ☐ NO Do I set standards for myself and others that are difficult to reach or maintain?

If you **answered yes to three or more of these questions,** there is a good chance you are still hurting from broken pieces in your life and could benefit from healing. I know it may seem impossible to see at this point, but this is NOT how your life is supposed to be, and denying your broken pieces will only cause further brokenness. Your denial will catch up to you if it hasn't already.

NOTES

_____

_____

_____

_____

_____

_____

_____

_____

_____

_____

_____

_____

_____

_____

_____

_____

_____

_____

_____

_____

_____

_____

"Until you understand there is beauty in your vulnerability, you will never be able to tell your story with your whole heart."

~KRIS REECE

4

Tear Down the Walls

Carpenters know to carefully examine the structure of a house before they start remodeling it into a dream home. In order to uncover any potential issues—such as faulty plumbing, termites or mold—they must tear down the walls and look inside. Sometimes the problems can be remedied; other times the entire structure needs to come down. But the only way to expose what needs to be addressed is to tear down the walls. Only then can they see just what it will take to bring a home to structural health.

The same goes for you. You typically can't see your emotional wounds because they hide behind the walls you've built to keep yourself going. But you certainly can feel and see their effects. And so, at some point, you must look inside and expose the wound behind the walls before you can remedy it and begin building your beautiful new life.

I know that this can be a scary proposition. But I assure you: **Whatever is revealed can be healed.** In fact, Jesus needs us to bring it into the light. Are you ready to stop hiding in darkness?

Let's tear down the walls.

❤ WILL THIS HURT?

I have yet to meet anyone who has skated through life without a scrape of some sort. Some injuries are superficial and only require a quick cleaning and a band-aid before you are back in action, while others are a little deeper. They may require a more thorough cleaning and a longer recovery period. Some even require stitches because the wound is so deep.

Think back to when you were a kid, when the thought of having your boo-boo cleaned was enough to bring tears to your eyes. You would have given anything to avoid it. But what you didn't realize at the time was that if you didn't go through the temporary discomfort, or even pain, an infection could set in, making the healing process significantly longer and much more painful.

Once, I was mountain biking in the beautiful mountains of Colorado. I was with a group of people, and we were all having a great time until I wiped out. It wasn't the worst crash ever, but it sure did hurt. My bike slipped as I was going down the mountain, and my body scraped against the jagged rocks for about 20 feet. As I rose to my feet in disgust, I realized I had several cuts all over my arms, hands and back. I had a choice to make. I could leave my group, turn around and get first aid, or I could suck it up and continue on.

As my friends can attest, I am a suck-it-up kinda gal. So I kept riding despite the discomfort. It was several hours before I arrived back at my hotel room, where I discovered that I had loose pieces of damaged skin attempting to adhere to the good skin that was left.

Fast forward several hours, and I am in a meeting. I see the area becoming red and inflamed. Only then did I realize that the loose skin needed to be cut away and the wound cleaned.

I had another choice to make: I could miss this very important meeting or I could get this wound taken care of. I found a happy medium, or so I thought. I went into the bathroom, cut

WHATEVER IS REVEALED CAN BE HEALED.

the skin off myself and cleaned and disinfected the open wound. Later that evening, the area started to turn black. *Uh oh,* I thought. As I poked around the wound, I discovered a small rock imbedded in my skin—hence, the blackness.

At this time of the night my only options were the emergency room or doing it myself. You guessed it: This suck-it-up gal dug the rock out herself and cleaned it all up again. It took a long time before that wound healed.

Had I just taken care of the minor wound from the start, it wouldn't have affected (or infected) my entire day. Sometimes there is a place for self-help; other times, we need a professional to help us see what we can't.

❤ CLEANING YOUR WOUNDS

My mountain biking story illustrates what happens when we allow emotional wounds to remain: They infect our everyday life by influencing the way we interact with people, places and things.

Much like I did with my physical wounds, most people try to ignore their emotional wounds. For example, you may think you're doing a good job, until one day you explode or break down. That's when people you love start saying, "What is wrong with you?" You suddenly discover you have a choice to make: continue trying to hide your wounds or get help.

At her husband's prompting, Kiera came to me for help regarding her anger. Kiera had just found out about an affair that John had two years ago. He admitted to sleeping with another woman once, but Kiera sensed there was more than that and she wanted the truth.

John asked her to seek counseling because he loved her and he wanted it to work—*Why won't she just get over this…it was in the past…can't we just move on?* Kiera responded in very destructive ways. When angry, Kiera would kick John out of the house, break his things and call him derogatory names. All of their friends sided with John, making Kiera feel like more of an outcast.

When I sat with Kiera she said, "Since he's making me come here, let me tell you what this scumbag did to me. I found evidence that he had an affair two years ago, and now he tells me all he did was sleep with her once. ALL HE DID? Even if that was all he did, that's still enough to make me want to slit his throat."

Kiera's emotions were clearly very high. After determining that "slit his throat" was figurative, we moved forward. "I know there's more he's not telling me. He wouldn't have even told me about this if I didn't find out."

Many people would label Kiera *a woman from hell* or *crazy*. But after spending some time with her, I could see why she was having such strong reactions. Kiera's trust had been broken as a young girl. Her father divorced her mother for another woman and left the home at a young age. Kiera's older brother poked fun at Kiera because she would cry over her dad leaving. He laughed at her, telling her that she was nothing but a sissy and that her dad didn't care about her anyway. This was extremely painful for Kiera to hear.

She desperately searched for acceptance in her school years and beyond. When rejected, Kiera responded in an inflamed manor, because she simply was never taught how to handle her emotions. Her parents' divorce and brother's behavior left a gaping wound that she never healed.

Now, with her trust broken again by the first man that she truly loved, she was frantic. Her core belief that no man could ever be trusted was triggered, and she was beside herself that she had allowed herself to be hurt in the same way all over again.

It took some time for Kiera to repair her trust wound. She had to re-experience some painful memories. She also had to take responsibility for her actions that were a result of her core beliefs. But she made it. Does she have scars? Yes, but scars don't hurt; it's wounds that are painful.

Kiera is still learning to trust, and her husband has

admitted his involvement with the other woman. They have both agreed to be honest with each other, and Kiera is practicing how to moderate her responses, making them more applicable to the situation.

As you get ready to tear down some of your walls, please remember that the process may hurt in the short-term. But if you allow yourself to experience the discomfort and work through the pain, the journey will be quicker. And the rewards on the other side are indescribable.

♥ ALLOW THE WALLS TO COME DOWN

The toughest part in this process is letting yourself be vulnerable. If you are like most people, you have lived with walls and armor for a long time, which you feel have protected you and kept you safe. And while that may be partially true—they've gotten you this far—at some point the walls and armor start to keep out more good than bad.

Tearing down the walls and removing the fortress of armor is going to make many of you feel naked and exposed. To the extent that you are able, embrace this feeling. (Or at least, agree to tolerate it.) I'm recalling 1 Peter 2:9, which my heart translates this way: "I am God's very own possession. As a result, I can show others the goodness of God, for he called me out of the darkness into his wonderful light." He loves you so much that He is longing for you to call all that is hidden in darkness behind walls out into His glorious light for healing. THEN you will be able to show others the goodness of God. Believe me, there is so much beauty waiting for you.

Do not go running behind the walls again. Let's work to see what's behind them, then bring them crumbling down.

Your Assignment
DISCOVER WHAT LIES BENEATH

Let's take a peek behind your walls.

STEP 1: Watch your words. This step is designed to help you get outside of yourself and listen to what you are saying. I remember a time when I was talking with friends and, for some reason, I started to actually hear myself as I was talking. Has this ever happened to you? It's a strange experience when it first happens. But it's as if you are listening to someone else's conversation—in my case, this person sounded like a sarcastic jerk. I thought I was being funny, but when I actually heard myself, I realized that's not how I sounded at all.

It all happened because I was able to listen to the words as they came out of my mouth. Now I have the ability to do this on command. And so can you, it just may take some practice. Try it with me. Put this book down and go start a conversation with the nearest person to you. Obviously you want to listen to what he or she is saying. But more importantly, you want to listen to what you are saying.

Welcome back! How did it go? What did you find out? Did you say silly, superficial fillers? Perhaps you made a few jokes. Maybe you made some derogatory comments about yourself or began to gossip about someone else. Whatever you discovered, you're getting the hang of listening to your own words.

Listening to yourself is a critically important habit to have in place before and to then draw on during your next difficult conversation or argument, since difficult conversations are where many automatic thoughts and core beliefs reveal themselves. It's going to be one of the biggest challenges of all. These squabbles are typically the times where it's easy to go into "core mode"—where core beliefs take over and do the talking. But it doesn't have to be this way.

Here's what I want you to do the next time you have an argument that takes on a life of its own. You know that argument: the one that starts off innocently enough but then your partner, in the course of explaining or defending himself, slaps one of your wounds. You feel your needs are not being met, and that's when those core beliefs start digging a deeper hole. STOP right there. Try to capture your words. What are you saying? If it all seems too much at the time, record your conversation. Not so you can catch your partner in the wrong; this is all for you. You must be able to listen to the words coming out of YOUR mouth.

Another way to go about this is to ask your partner or someone you interact with on a regular basis: "What is something I do or say that leaves you puzzled or irritated after our conversation?"

Your job? Just listen. This is not a time to defend yourself or get upset about what they say. Thank them and consider it a shortcut. They are giving you the blueprint to discovery. Take what they've said and try to hear it coming out of your own mouth.

Here's an example of someone who didn't realize how her words were creating her own unhappiness:

Lori, a young ad executive, climbed the corporate ladder quickly due to her finesse. However, her co-workers all had a common complaint about her: She was always so defensive. Everyone walked on eggshells when it came to sharing their constructive criticism with Lori. She would start defending herself and often blame others before the person was done explaining how she could improve. This attitude spilled over into her personal life, but she brushed it off by saying, "No man can keep up with me." At the office, everyone was wrong and "jealous" (her words).

It wasn't until Lori stopped getting the promotions she expected that she came to me for help. It took her some time to recognize that she was being defensive and not allowing others to speak. Looking back, Lori had issues with control in her past. She struggled with perfectionist beliefs, and she attacked others in an effort to not feel like a failure. The result? No one could get close to Lori, further solidifying her belief that she had to be perfect to be loved.

STEP 2: Honestly assess the damage. Just like the contractor peering into an open wall, you are going to need an accurate assessment of the problem. When a carpenter discovers mold, he doesn't say, "Oh that stinks, let me put up a new wall and call it good." That would be ludicrous. No, he completely eradicates the mold before he rebuilds the structure. Doesn't that make sense? Left alone, the mold would eat through the new wall eventually.

The same is true of leaving faulty thinking and dysfunctional core beliefs behind the wall. It's only a matter of time before the infestation resurfaces again. It's time to be honest. I'm talking no makeup, walls down, honest. You already feel naked and vulnerable, but remember you're safe here. You have a loving God to meet you right where you are, but He needs and requires your honesty.

If you keep hiding, you are not only fooling yourself,

you may also be cutting yourself off from God. "But your iniquities have separated you from your God; your sins have hidden his face from you, so that he will not hear." (Isaiah 59:2)

I understand this sounds harsh, but God can only deal with and heal what you bring into the light. Everything in darkness is hidden from Him. He's waiting for you to expose it. This is a sign of honesty and surrender before Him.

Let's review what you've accomplished so far. Your journey began with identifying the wounds in your life. For some, those wounds were easy to identify, because they are constantly on the forefront of your mind. For others, it took a little while to step out of denial and discover what has left you wounded.

Next, you took the time to search for your core beliefs. Doing so is not always easy, as core beliefs like to hide deep and sneak-attack when least expected. The process of identifying recurring thoughts and overreactions was an important part of this process.

Then, you answered some questions to uncover your broken pieces.

Hang in there with me: I promise this all ties together to help you understand to what exactly you have been prisoner.

STEP 3: Look back with love. The next step is to revert back into little-girl-mode. It's time to break out the photos. Find pictures of yourself from the following age groups:

- Preschool years
- Grades one through four (age 5-8)
- Grades five through eight (age 8-14)

- High school years (age 15-18)
- Post-high school or college (age 18-22)
- Marriage or dating (age 22+)
- Present time

First get into prayer and ask the Holy Spirit to open your eyes to see what He is longing to reveal and heal in your life. Ask for the strength and patience to persevere through this process. Now fix yourself a cup of tea, grab a note pad, and find a quiet place to spend some time with these photos. Pretend you are being interviewed and these are the questions:

1. Tell me about this girl.
2. What were her hopes and dreams?
3. What was she dealing with at this stage?
4. What were her fears?

As you work through the questions and the stages of your life, write down what is revealed to you. I had one woman working through this process break down in tears; she felt compelled to apologize to the little girl in one of her pictures. She apologized to her for the adults in her life that did not love her the way she needed to be loved. She assured the little girl in that picture that those adults did the best they could. She began to see that little girl in the picture as the lovable little girl that God created her to be, and her walls began to crumble.

Then, compare photos from the present to these pictures from the past. More often than not, the answers to the questions are very similar, IF you are being honest. Remember, it's pointless to do this if you aren't going to be honest. There can be no healing without truth.

Finally, connect the dots. It is freedom that you are truly seeking, yes? Freedom from the walls that keep love out. Freedom from being trapped between two people—the one you are and the one you want to be. Freedom from the chains that feel like they are slowly choking the life out of you. And freedom from the phony facades that not even you believe anymore. I know it is freedom you long for. Keep going!

Take all of the answers that you compiled and circle or highlight common themes: words that are repeated. For example, *fear*, or *scared* or *angry*—you get the idea.

"THEN YOU WILL KNOW THE TRUTH, AND THE TRUTH WILL SET YOU FREE." (JOHN 8:32)

It's not uncommon for the devil—the enemy of our soul—to have us feeling so overwhelmed that we think we can't possibly address everything that needs our attention in order for us to heal (more on this in Chapter 5). But often our thoughts are the same thing repeating itself in different ways. Your enemy would love nothing more than for you to remain in this muck and confusion and never find your way out. You can find your freedom. Remember: Everything that comes from his lips to your ears is a lie.

STEP 4: Lay down your hammer. If you have walked through these steps with care, I know you are exhausted and hoping to take a break. But stay with me, as this is the best part.

It's time to surrender. The fighting is over. The battle is finished. Your loving Father in Heaven is telling you that He will finish this fight for you.

Put your tea away and take the list that you created from the answered questions. Your job is to focus on those common themes, the repeated words that I had you look for earlier.

It's time to simplify and be set free.

With your words in hand, go back to your Loving Father and get honest. He will not hurt you. He will not punish you. He wants you to be all that He created you to be.

It's time to pray. I suggest you begin with praising Him for being the awesome God that He is. I suggest you thank Him for loving you so much that He will not leave you in the state that you are in. Exclaim to Him that you believe that He holds your healing and your future. Release to Him all of the areas that are circled on your list. Admit to Him all that you have struggled with and are currently struggling with. Repent of the ways in which you tried to correct these issues yourself, only making a further mess.

Than lay them down as a sign of surrender and ask Him to help you through the healing process. Ask Him to make you into the woman He wants you to be.

This is a prayer and release from a woman in my practice named Laila.

> *Dear God, I know in my head you are a great God, but I am afraid to admit it in my heart. I know you are an awesome God with mighty powers, and I know that you love me. Why, I don't know, but I know that you do. As I've looked*

back over my life, God, I realize that I have been plagued with never feeling good enough. I have struggled with a fear of financial failure. I ask you to forgive me today for all the ways that I have tried to manage these fears on my own. I made matters worse and closed myself off from the great and mighty plans that you have for my life. I want to release them today into your power and ask for your help. I believe that I am good enough. Because you created me, I believe that you will provide all of my needs. I believe all of this in my head, God, please help it travel to my heart. I am in your hands completely. Amen.

Can you do that? I know you can. Our Heavenly Father made getting right with Him so simple that even a child can do it. The problem is, we have built so many walls to make us appear as if we have it all together that we have buried our childlike faith.

Now it's time for those walls to come down.

"The enemy is nowhere near as powerful as the words spoken against oneself."

~KRIS REECE

5
Overcome Common Obstacles to Healing

We all have enemies in this world—obstacles to healing. The first one that I want to discuss is an enemy you cannot physically see, but you can certainly see the effects of his attacks: Satan. Although he is nowhere near as powerful as our God, when you allow his attempts to shake you, you give him enough power to wreak havoc in your life.

This enemy wants to keep you from all that God has in store for you. When your life feels like a constant fight, remember the words of Paul in the book of Ephesians 6:12 (NIV): "For our struggle is not against flesh and blood, but against the rulers, against the authorities, against the powers of this dark world and against the spiritual forces of evil in the heavenly realms."

Believe it or not, you are in control of how much power Satan exerts on your life. Yes, for all you control freaks out there, you can control this danger! How? Two ways:

The first is with your words. As Proverbs 6:2 says, we are snared by the words of our mouth. So be very careful what you say to yourself. Remember the saying your mother taught you, "If you have nothing nice to say, then say nothing at all"? The same applies when you're talking to you. When you speak words of negativity to yourself, you give Satan and his minions the power to bring forth that which you have just spoken.

Take Clarisa, for example. Clarisa has struggled with low self-esteem her entire life. Her core belief is that whoever she is in relationship with will eventually reject her. Her fears drive her. She fears she will say something stupid, fears that people will see the mistakes she makes and judge her for them, fears that she won't be able to fulfill others' needs.

When Clarisa was shown Job 3:25—"What I feared has come upon me; what I dreaded has happened to me"— her eyes opened. She said, "You mean, all this time it has been fear that has opened the door for all of this to happen?"

Yes, that's exactly what happened. Her core beliefs made her fearful. Fear is one of the biggest weapons Satan uses to trap you. That's right, TRAP you! Once you have given in to fear, you have more faith in what Satan can do than what God can do, and now he has legal right to do what he wants. You can bet that he will capitalize on this opportunity and bring it to pass.

Satan derives tremendous joy from making you question God. But when he gets credit for pain you inflict on yourself, that's a bonus for him.

My point is, not all of what is holding you back comes from Satan. Your second worst enemy is your own mind.

Sometimes, long after Satan's work is done, we take over on the project and continue his dirty work. He plants the seeds, and we continue to water them with negative self-talk. And worse, we seem to never even question the garbage that bounces around in our mind and comes out of our mouth. We act like zombies and repeat whatever foolishness we have been told.

How many times do you shake your head at someone (especially a young adult) who is just spouting something that you know they heard from their parents or friends? Their ignorance is so obvious, yet they speak with such confidence. Why? Because they believe it. They never thought to question what they heard. That's the same thing that happens when negative thoughts enter our heads and come out of our mouths. We don't seem to question them.

Sam grew up a very bright, curious young boy, traits that caused him to frequently have clumsy little accidents. He had an active mind that moved far faster than his hands or words could express, so he often fumbled over things.

Sam's father used to poke fun at him, making him very insecure. He would say things like, "Would you watch what you're doing, you idiot?" Or, "Only girls act that clumsy and get away with it. Are you a girl, Sam?"

These thoughts stayed with Sam his entire life. While in the break room at work, if he would bump into a chair or spill a little sugar outside of his coffee mug (as many of us do), he would uncontrollably apologize and say derogatory comments about himself—statements like, "Oh, I'm such a klutz, I think my parents made a mistake and I was supposed to be a girl." He thought he was being humorous and deflecting attention away from his clumsiness, but in fact he was solidifying in his own mind the comments made about him from his childhood.

So, how can you tell if it is Satan attacking you or if your own thoughts that are binding you up? Here are a few questions to ask yourself:

- **Am I in the will of God?** Sometimes the things we go through in life can be challenging, but they are not attacks. In fact they are more likes tests, designed to promote you, not fail you. Ask yourself: Do I have any areas of rebellion in my life? Is there something I know that I should be doing or not doing that I am choosing to ignore? If the answer is yes, this is not a test to promote you; this is the work of Satan. It doesn't come from God.

- **Did I give the enemy a foothold anywhere?** Meaning, do the words you speak about yourself and others line up with the Word of God? Are you saying what He says about you and your life? If not, you are most likely giving a foothold for the enemy to operate in your life. Clean up all of your inconsistent talk, both about yourself and others. If you are the type to speak God's word over your life but gossip about others, you're opening a door for demonic attack. If you are speaking God's word, but it's followed by a complaint or negativity, you are not in the will of God and you are opening the door wide open for your words to come to life.

- **Where did the thought come from?** This may take a little detective work, but it's worth it. Did this thought come out of nowhere? Then it's most likely from your adversary. Has this thought been mulling around in your mind, or was it triggered by something someone made you feel? Then it's more likely from a core belief of yours that needs to be changed. Don't be mistaken: Satan can play off of your core beliefs about yourself, too. Sadly, these are the ones we believe so easily.

Regardless of where the thought or attack is coming from, you have the power to use it positively. I am not saying it will be easy; in fact, it will be the most difficult time of your life to speak positive things about yourself that you don't quite believe yet—things that may even make you feel like a fool and a phony—but give it a try. God will show up and step in!

♥ 6 COMMON WAYS YOU MAY BE KEEPING YOURSELF STUCK

Women have much to battle against for their freedom and happiness. We battle more in the spirit realm—as Paul references—than we realize. But we also need to understand how we hold ourselves back.

Here's a glimpse into what we, as women, have to deal with in our society, and how those obstacles can keep us stuck and unhappy.

1. **Image.** Perhaps you had a string of break-ups, or perhaps you didn't land the dream job you thought you were perfect for. Sometimes it's difficult to pinpoint the exact event or events that led you to question yourself and your confidence. All you know is that now you're looking around and noticing that other women are a bit more attractive than you. You see that others share your same talent yet are perhaps more gifted than you are.

At some point, you realize that you're not quite as perfect as you thought you were when you were younger. Perhaps, at some point, you decided to hide behind an image instead of taking a clear-eyed look at where you've gotten off track and doing what it takes to mend your broken parts. This image could be based upon what society tells you you should be doing, looking like or acting like. It could be based upon some image conjured up in your own mind.

And why not hide behind an image? You rarely see a post on social media that says, "Feeling insecure this morning" or "My marriage is failing, and it's my fault." Rather, people put only their best out there. As a result, everyone appears to have their act together, always looking good in their photos and are constantly getting rave reviews from their "friends."

Instead of getting a sneak peek into someone's "real" life, social media shows you only what a person chooses for you to see. Of course it's going to be good. But if you are struggling with insecurity or inadequacy, you are left feeling that there must be something wrong with you. And instead of recognizing that no one is sharing the whole truth, or getting help for this faulty way of thinking, you pull out all the stops to make sure that the image you portray is a positive one. You want everyone to believe you married your best friend and that you have the best kids EVER, who succeed at everything they do. What a farce!

Once you create an image, you have to maintain it. So the lie continues. Yes, I said lie, because that's what it truly is. Whether you are saying it to someone else or yourself, it's a lie. It's a lie to believe that if you can maintain an image then all is well.

Image is only good when it comes from who you are in Christ. When it is a self-made image, it is on sinking sand, and it's one of the main reasons women stay stuck. Why do the work to break free into something wonderful when you've convinced yourself you are fine?

2. **Fear.** This is a biggie. Fear comes in many forms, but in every instance it disguises itself well. It hides behind past experiences, future uncertainties and voices of confusion. Although it is evasive, fear is very real, whether you want to admit it or not. I have yet to counsel or coach a person whose reason for not moving forward didn't stem, at least in part, from fear—yet they each had 12 other excuses for why they were stuck. It takes everyone a certain amount of time to realize that the thing that's holding them back is actually fear.

Fear is a motivator for some (and not in a good way), a debilitator for others and a demon for most. If there was anything good about fear, I doubt we would have 365 examples in the Bible for us to "fear not."

We face fear on a daily basis, but whether we kneel to it, buy it a drink or kick it to the curb is the difference between healing and stuckness, between a new life and old pain. Fear comes in many forms:

- You may fear the pain, the work or the discomfort you will have to experience to get through what is holding you back. Regardless of how long I do this work, it still amazes me when people choose to leave their pain buried inside instead of taking a short, bumpy train ride to freedom. They become almost overwhelmed by the process.

- Perhaps you fear failure. It's always easier to talk about what you would do than to actually do it, because there is a chance that it may not work out. Talking about what you want to do or talking about the reasons why you can't do something right now is always safer than doing it and failing. I know you've heard the saying "Failure is not an option." For many, that motto is a motivator to do everything possible to achieve their goals. Others think if failure is not an option, they won't try.

- Fear of rejection may be keeping you stuck. It may seem easier to stay where you are and curl up with your excuses than risk the pain of rejection. Rejection may be a pain you're just not willing to face or, sadly, even contemplate. But if you can't even acknowledge a feeling, you're going to have a near-impossible time moving beyond it.

Rejection is everywhere. Is it even possible for everyone, everywhere to like everything we do? When you think in logical terms, your mind tells you *of course not, that's impossible.* So why do you get depressed or obsessed when anyone, anywhere doesn't like something you do?

Everyone will face rejection. The difference between a secure person and an insecure person is how they handle it and use it.

- Fear of the unknown is a very common reason to stay stuck. You may have ideas about where you'd like to be. You may even say, "Wouldn't it be nice if…" But if you're like the majority of people, you'd rather accept your current reality than change the status quo in the hopes of something better.

This way of thinking keeps so many women stuck at dead-end jobs, dating losers and not fulfilling their dreams. It breaks my heart when I see this because for some no matter how bad the situation is (and for some it's bad), they feel deep inside that this may be the best they'll get, and if they move away from it they will only find worse. (This is related to a deeper self-esteem issue that we will talk about later.)

Remember, God did not give you a spirit of fear, but of power, love and self-discipline. Everything you need to get unstuck is already in you.

3. **Dreams.** Dreams are another reason many women stay stuck in the muck. Yes, dreams are great to have. Without dreams how do you know what you long for?

But dreams without a plan are nothing more than a wish. They have no backbone, no structure. They have nothing to support them and help them grow. And that's the peril of the dreamer mindset—it keeps you out of touch with reality. The dreamers I see in my practice have done nothing with the resources they have. And what amazes me is that some of them have truly great resources, but their mentality holds them back from ever getting started.

Dreamers are the ones who wait for "Mr. Right" to come knocking on the door. These are the people who keeping praying for God to show them their purpose instead of getting out there and helping in every way they can. These are the people who are waiting for the perfect job, but if you ask their employers, they are turning in only an average performance.

Dreamers constantly hear stories of others becoming an overnight success—a singer getting discovered in a bar or a millionaire who stumbled into his success—and imagine that it could happen to them too someday. What they fail to see is that every one of those success stories is a hard worker who has done and continues to do all they can to be all they came to be.

I've never heard of anyone who spends most of her time sitting on a barstool talking about her dreams becoming an overnight success. I've never heard of someone becoming a multi-millionaire by talking about what she would do if it were her business. That's because dreamers dream and doers do. Keep dreaming but start adding some "doing" to your day and watch yourself begin to see some of your dreams come true.

4. **Faulty thinking.** It's exactly what it implies—there is something wrong in the thought process. Thoughts lead to actions, so if your thought process is broken, your actions will be broken, too.

Think of Proverbs 23:7: "For as a man thinks in his heart, so is he." If you are constantly dwelling on negative thoughts, you'll get negative actions as a result.

I'm sure you know someone who can always find a reason why something can't be done. If you ask what can be done, she can't even go there. Her mind has been so fixed on the negative for so long that she can't even seem to conjure up a positive solution without slapping it down in her mind before it even makes it to her mouth.

If this is you, I want to challenge you to ponder 2 Corinthians 10:5: "We demolish arguments and every pretension that sets itself up against the knowledge of God, and we take captive every thought to make it obedient to Christ."

In other words, God's not a fan of stinkin' thinkin'! Recall the story of the Little Engine that Could and recite his encouraging words: "I think I can, I think I can." These words encouraged children everywhere to think positively and to keep moving. How unappealing would the story have been if we listened to this little engine list every reason why something wouldn't work and stubbornly stay stuck in his reasons?

5. **Second-guessing.** You may want so much to move forward; you know the desires of your heart, but you allow confusion to set in. The result? Constant second-guessing and missed opportunities.

You may even go so far as to assume that it wasn't the will of God or "not meant to be" when something doesn't work out—as if God is going to make you come to the right decision. How many times have you been stuck in the vacillation process? I know I have, countless times. Going back and forth, changing my mind, running through the what ifs, then finally coming to a decision only to flip-flop for the fifth time in an hour.

You may actually think you are being humble and holy in this process, and justify it by saying that you don't want to miss God.

I have news for you: If God is the greatest navigator of your life and He guides your path (Proverbs 3:6) and directs your steps (Psalm 37:23), don't you think He can get you back on course if you veer off? And if you are listening to Him the way you should, then you won't veer too far. He will even use the detour you took to your advantage and His glory!

6. **The past.** The fifth reason why you may stay stuck is that you are using your past to determine your present and future. It may be conscious, or you may not even realize what you're doing.

Think back to when you were a child or a young adult: You were unstoppable, you dreamed big, you loved hard and you sang loud. Now, after life has slapped you around, handed you a few failure notices and laughed at you on more than one occasion, you don't attack things with the same voraciousness. Now, you use past setbacks as a benchmark for what's going to happen in your future.

We've all made mistakes. We've all been embarrassed and hurt in one way or another, but none of these occurrences have to dictate our future. Many studies have proven that people succeed when they already think they are a success. I would like you to try this little experiment. Read the following paragraph, imagining it's about you, then close your eyes and observe how you feel:

Your parents unfortunately weren't your real parents. They rescued you from a hospital because your mother was a prostitute who overdosed on drugs and your father was already in prison. Not wanting you to grow up under those conditions, these people took you in and raised you as their own.

What are you feeling right now? What do you think you would start feeling as the days and weeks went on? With those actually in this situation, some feel grateful that they were taken from such an unfortunate circumstance and given a loving home. They move on with their lives not thinking much about the parents who left them behind or their connection to them. But most feel a sense of worthlessness. They question genetics and their family tree. They start to identify themselves with the negative traits of their biological parents. Their self-esteem becomes challenged and their lives an uphill battle.

Now close your eyes again and do the same thing for the next scenario:

Your parents unfortunately weren't your real parents. They adopted you because your biological parents were killed in a car accident. But now you've discovered that your biological parents were actually royalty and your biological grandparents want to honor you just the same.

What are you feeling right now? If this was you, how do you think those feelings would begin to determine how you act later on? Do you think you'd walk around with you head hung low or would you hold your head high?

Let's come back to reality. In both situations, YOU never changed. You were still you. You were still from the same upbringing, and you still had the same experiences. The only thing that changed is what you thought about yourself.

Your past can be used to your advantage or disadvantage. You can use it as a tool or an excuse, as a launching pad or handcuffs. It truly is your choice how you view your past.

This is your life, and it's not over. I know the thought of dredging up the past and working through issues that you thought you buried long ago is enough to make you hide under the covers like a scared little girl—or open a second bottle of wine like a grown-up little girl. I know it can be overwhelming.

But you have many years left—how do you want to live them? Let's say you're 50 years old and let's say it took you two years to work through your issues. Think about how many years of your life that still leaves for you to enjoy your newfound joy and freedom.

I promise you it's worth the journey.

NOTES

*"On Christ the solid Rock
I stand, all other ground
is sinking sand."*

~EDWARD MOTE

6
Is the Foundation Faulty?

You wouldn't dream of building a home on a faulty foundation. Without a strong, solid base, it'd be just a matter of time before the structure crashed to the ground.

The same holds true for the expectations we have in life. If we want love, we can't build on a foundation of hate and revenge. If we want peace, we can't build on a foundation of strife and defensiveness. If we want emotional health, we can't build on a foundation of faulty thoughts and beliefs.

It's time to get crystal clear about the foundation you have built your life upon.

Your Assignment
USE A JOURNAL TO GET CLARITY ON YOUR THOUGHTS AND FEELINGS

I love the old saying, "If you want to see what something is made of, put it in hot water." We all have our breaking points. Some of us get triggered quicker than others. The purpose here is not to find fault in how soon you break, rather to determine your breaking point and how you respond.

Journaling is an incredible tool that can illuminate how everyday situations trigger unhelpful thoughts and unpleasant feelings. You can write as much or as little as you want, but your primary instruction is to write down every situation that bothers you, and capture as many of your thoughts about them as you can.

Don't filter here. Give as much detail as possible. I would rather you write about two or three situations and dig deep than write about 20 situations in little detail.

For example, you may be angry that your husband didn't pick up his socks off the floor, but feel silly writing something so trivial down. It doesn't matter how big or justifiable an offense is. In fact, it's the little stuff that we tend to push aside that typically holds the most information.

The start to an entry may look something like this:

Situation: My boss added more work to my already full plate. I just talked to him last week about this.

Or

Situation: My son didn't even call to wish me a happy Mother's Day.

A LIST OF
Common Feelings

It should be fairly easy to capture the thoughts running around your head and commit them to paper. You simply have to listen and resist the urge to edit. Identifying your feelings requires a bit more skill, as most of us have had very little in the way of an emotional education.

To help, here's a list of common feelings that could describe your emotional state:

Accepting	Angry	Adoring
Afraid	Amazed	Annoyed
Anticipating	Anxious	Apprehensive
Aroused	Ashamed	Blue
Bored	Calm	Cheerful
Confident	Content	Delighted
Depressed	Disappointed	Distracted
Disgusted	Ecstatic	Elated
Embarrassed	Energetic	Enraged
Enthused	Euphoric	Excited
Exuberant	Frustrated	Grieved
Guilty	Happy	Hateful
Hopeless	Hostile	Humiliated
Hungry	Hurt	Intense
Jealous	Joyful	Loving
Moody	Nervous	Peaceful
Sad	Sick	Surprised
Terrified	Tranquil	Troubled
Watchful	Worried	Zestful

The situation you begin with doesn't matter. What matters is that you track what happens next.

For each triggering event, write down the thoughts and feelings that accompany it. This is the time to be detailed, candid and raw. Holding back won't help you gain new clarity. This process will begin to reveal the faults in your foundation—the underlying thoughts that drive much of how you react to people and situations.

Take Eric: Eric has struggled his entire life with insecurity. He has been cheated on by every girlfriend and wife. He spent a good number of years in counseling prior to our meeting, and he talked of the tremendous gains he made in understanding why he was choosing unfaithful women. "When my insecurity rises up, I say some of the most foolish things."

Eric was tired of ignoring the fact that he would leave his wife a voicemail then not hear back from her for hours. "I know she has clients that she is working with and probably can't get to the phone. I just hate where my mind goes and I can't focus on anything else," he told me. The effects were debilitating.

But when Eric took the time to walk through this situation, he was able to uncover the thoughts and feelings it was triggering:

Thought: If she loved me she would call me back right away. *Feeling:* I feel like a fool.

Thought: I wonder if someone else has caught her eye. *Feeling:* I feel inferior.

Thought: I can't do enough to hold on to her. *Feeling:* I feel inadequate and pressured.

Journal Entries SAMPLE

Situation: My husband came in hugging and kissing me.

Thoughts: There aren't enough hours in a day. I know my husband wants sex. I just don't feel it right now, but I know how sad he gets if I let him down. I think I am the worst wife for not giving my husband sex when he wants it. He'll probably end up cheating on me someday.

Feelings: Anxious, frustrated, guilty

In the case of this woman, her husband loves her very much and would not stray from their marriage. But she is interpreting his advances instead of talking to him about it, causing her to carry anxiety and guilt inside.

* * * * *

Situation: A coworker went behind my back to get a project approved and now I have to deal with the problems it created.

Thoughts: I clearly am not worthy of respect if someone goes behind my back to get something done. I am the biggest witch if I say anything. I will just disregard her so she knows that I am angry. If people don't apologize then they don't really care about me—since no one ever apologizes, people don't really care about me.

Feelings: Angry, disgusted, disrespected

This woman thought she had control over her emotions simply because she didn't explode on people, but she carried around a tremendous amount of anger and malice in her heart that seeped out into her interactions with people. All she wanted was to be appreciated and accepted, but her thoughts drove her actions, which in turn got negative reactions from others—further confirming her automatic thoughts.

Thought: I am a good man, but she can't see it. *Feeling:* I feel angry.

How many times do thoughts of everything you need to accomplish bounce around in your mind, causing your stress levels to rise in worry you've forgotten something? Letting those thoughts run amok creates more stress than the actual items on your to-do list.

When you have a lot to do, you know you often feel better just by listing and organizing your tasks, even if you haven't begun to tackle them yet. The same is true for your feelings. Getting them out and organized can give you a palpable sense of relief, because you no longer have to hold them in your mind. You can rest, knowing that you'll get to them when you're ready.

❤ WHAT TO WATCH OUT FOR

Keep a few things in mind as you journal:

- Monitor additional feelings that arise as a result of your original feelings. Sometimes we don't realize that the thoughts and feelings we have create other thoughts and feelings. For example, guilt is one of the strongest sub-feelings. If you feel disgusted at someone, another immediate feeling you might have is guilt for even feeling that way. This now leaves you with two feelings that can produce two separate thought patterns, or they can be interwoven into one.

- Be aware of anticipation: Sometimes it's not an actual occurrence that causes unpleasant thoughts and feelings, but the anticipation of a situation or a person's reactions that can cause feelings, which lead to thoughts.

- Remember, the point of these exercises is to raise your awareness of how your typical reactions dictate your reality. Only when you can clearly see your go-to thoughts and feelings can you choose a different path for yourself!

NOTES

"Trust in the Lord with all your heart, and do not lean on your own understanding. In all your ways acknowledge Him, and He will make straight your paths."

~PROVERBS **3:5-6**

7

God Is the Master Builder

If there is one thing I wish I could give everyone in the world, it would be to help them understand how loved they are by Christ, and how unlimited their potential for happiness is when they allow Him into their life. The healing that you work through in this book may bring about some lovely, albeit relatively minor, changes when used as a self-help guide alone. But supernatural healing can take place when you invite Jesus into your life.

In the last chapter, you revealed the thoughts and feelings that have been your unstable foundation up until this point. Now it's time to start rebuilding. But we're going to invite Jesus to play the role of the general contractor, because you don't want to rebuild with the same faulty materials, do you?

I didn't think so.

I don't know about you, but I am always up for a good challenge. If you have read this far, you too are a fighter, and fighters don't give up. They push through incredible adversity to see what's on the other side. Sometimes fighters don't even know there is another side; they just know that they must push forward.

It takes courage and trust to move forward in the midst of an uncomfortable time. Pray and invite God into the process, and let's take the next step.

USE GOD'S WORD TO CHECK YOUR THOUGHTS AND FEELINGS

As a human being, you have tremendous control over what you think. And still, so many people are enslaved by the ideas bouncing around in their mind. For every thought pattern, God has guidance. Without knowing, you have no ammunition to fight those negative core beliefs and thoughts that are used to having full dominion over your inner environment.

In this chapter, we're going to look at what God has to say about some of the most common destructive thoughts and emotions. It's important to read through these and let them sink into your mind and heart now, when you're clear and focused; the midst of an emotional storm is not the best time to start your research. By doing your homework at this point, you'll be prepared to keep your thoughts in line with God whenever your core beliefs are triggered.

Here's a story to illustrate just how transformative this work can be:

Young Olivia came to me because she was having trouble saying no to people, especially those closest to her. She spent much of her time doing things she didn't really want to do, and feeling guilty about it, because someone else—mainly her mother—insisted. When we first met, Olivia was even considering going to school to pursue a profession she had no interest in because her mother was insistent.

One particular conversation with her mother perfectly captures Olivia's typical thought cycle: Olivia asked her mother if she could spend time with her father. Her mother made her feel guilty for even asking—as if Olivia were betraying her mother by choosing her father over her. Olivia dropped the question, giving the mother what she wanted but leaving Olivia with a lot of unresolved feelings.

When Olivia began to journal those emotions, she discovered that she felt like a bad person for letting her mother down. She feared being rejected by the very person who was supposed to love her. Worse yet, Olivia had no ammunition to fight the manipulation and guilt swirling around in her confused mind.

Olivia and I worked together to find scripture that helped her identify and cope with these unpleasant feelings. The chart on the following pages shows our process: how we identified her current thoughts and the feelings underneath them, then found scripture to help her create new, true, more empowering thoughts.

Thoughts	I am the worst daughter ever.
Feelings	I feel worthless.
God's Word	"How precious are your thoughts about me, O God? They cannot be numbered!" (Psalm 139:17)
New Thoughts	I am like a precious diamond. I love my mother but I don't have to please people to feel worthy of their love. I can't "make" my mother feel better by doing what she wants to do. I have to live the life God gave me.

Thoughts	I am horrible for betraying my mother.
Feelings	I feel disconnected and discarded.
God's Word	"So be strong and courageous! Do not be afraid and do not panic before them. For the LORD your God will personally go ahead of you. He will neither fail you nor abandon you." (Deuteronomy 3:16)
New Thoughts	I am not trash, I am God's princess. If someone wants to threaten to discard me because I won't do what they say, I will let God fight that battle. I will not be made to feel bad. It's bad that they are trying to make me feel bad.

Thoughts	I don't appreciate my mother.
Feelings	I feel guilty.
God's Word	"For the weapons of our warfare are not carnal, but mighty through God to the pulling down of strongholds; Casting down imaginations, and every high thing that exalts itself against the knowledge of God, and bringing into captivity every thought to the obedience of Christ." (2 Corinthians 10:4-5)
New Thoughts	I didn't do anything wrong, so I will fight the enemy in my mind and not allow it to make me feel bad for something I didn't do. If I sin against God, I will repent, but I will not allow anyone to make me feel guilty and bad about something that is not a sin. I will love, but I will not be manipulated.

Some unpleasant feelings do come from God, but we must test them. In Olivia's case, did she do anything wrong? No. She was experiencing the effects of her mother's manipulative behavior. Her mother knew how much Olivia didn't like to disappoint her. She used this knowledge to make Olivia feel bad about herself.

Olivia learned the difference between convictions from the Holy Spirit and guilt that others use to get what they want. In doing so, she was able to move on to the next step in the process: rewriting her own story.

Your Assignment
FAMILIARIZE YOURSELF WITH COMMON FEELINGS AND GOD'S ANTIDOTE TO THEM

It's time to take your tracking to the next level. Refer back to the list of situations, feelings and thoughts you created in the last chapter, and begin to dig into God's word. (I have created a Blank Journal Page to help you do so-- please turn to page 146 in the appendix to find it.) When doing this, consider these words from our Loving Father: "You will seek me and find me when you seek me with all your heart." (Jeremiah 29:13)

Seek Him like you are seeking a sale on shoes, and you will find what He has to say about you and your situation.

There are many great references out there that have simplified this process for you. One book that helps my clients tremendously is Joyce Meyer's *The Secret Power of Speaking God's Word.* This little purple book is packed with feelings and situations that are easy to reference, and you can immediately find out what God has to say about each one. I have also included a list of Scripture Remedies for Common Negative Thoughts in the appendix of this book—please turn to page 139 to use it.

Once you find out what God has to say, you can apply His insight to your particular situation to inform your new response. When interpreting or creating a new response, I encourage you to step away from your emotions. Do like guys do and put those feelings in a separate compartment for now. With them out of the way, you will be able to look at your situation more objectively and more effectively contribute to a new response. Some women find it helpful to pretend that they are giving the new response as advice to a friend.

It's not easy to build something out of broken pieces. That's why I encourage you to let the word of God wash over you until you no longer "feel" what you previously felt. This takes time. Have patience with yourself in this process. Refer to what the Apostle Paul wrote in Romans 12:2: "And do not be conformed to this world, but be transformed by the renewing of your mind, that you may prove what is that good and acceptable and perfect will of God."

It does not say the "renewal of your mind" as if it's a one and done act. This is a process.

There's no denying that it takes tremendous practice. The same holds true for playing a sport. No one just shows up for a game and that's it; they spend an enormous amount of time in preparation beforehand. You cannot expect to be prepared to win the game if you never practice.

But when we do our part and allow God to do His part, we are transformed into something more beautiful than we could ever have created on our own.

NOTES

"Those blocks in your life can either be building blocks or stumbling blocks.

~PATTI KING MAJESKI

8

The Building Blocks

An elderly carpenter was ready to retire, so he told his boss of his plans to live a more leisurely life with his wife. He would miss the paycheck and would only barely get by without it, but he needed to slow down and relax. The contractor said he'd be sorry to see such a good worker go, and he asked the carpenter to build just one more house as a personal favor.

The carpenter said yes, but his heart was not in his work. He resorted to shoddy workmanship and used inferior materials. When the carpenter finished his work, the contractor came to inspect the house. He handed the front-door key to the carpenter. "This is your house," the contractor said. "It's my gift to you."

The carpenter was shocked! If he had only known he was building his own house, he would have done it all so differently.

You are the carpenter of your life. Each day you hammer a nail, place a board,or erect a wall. Your attitudes and the choices you make today build your tomorrow.

What kind of work are you putting into building your life? Are you like the carpenter, building with lesser materials and doing shoddy work?

THE CHOICES YOU MAKE TODAY BUILD YOUR TOMORROW.

Maybe you put a phony smile on your face and convince yourself that you feel great. But those lies aren't quality materials; it will only be a matter of time before your structure cracks, falls or crumbles. In order to allow the Lord to build something beautiful from your broken pieces, you must use these three key building blocks:

♥ FORGIVENESS

Then Peter came and said to Him, "Lord, how often shall my brother sin against me, and I forgive him? Until seven times?"

Jesus said to him, "I don't tell you until seven times, but, until seventy times seven. Therefore the Kingdom of Heaven is like a certain king, who wanted to reconcile accounts with his servants. When he had begun to reconcile, one was brought to him who owed him ten thousand talents. But because he couldn't pay, his lord commanded him to be sold, with his wife, his children, and all that he had, and payment to be made. The servant therefore fell down and knelt before him, saying, 'Lord, have patience with me, and I will repay you all!' The lord of that servant, being moved with compassion, released him, and forgave him the debt.

"But that servant went out, and found one of his fellow servants, who owed him one hundred denarii, and he grabbed him, and took him by the throat, saying, 'Pay me what you owe!'

So his fellow servant fell down at his feet and begged him, saying, 'Have patience with me, and I will repay you!' He would not, but went and cast him into prison, until he should pay back that which was due. So when his fellow servants saw what was done, they were exceedingly sorry, and came and told to their lord all that was done. Then his lord called him in, and said to him, 'You wicked servant! I forgave you all that debt, because you begged me. Shouldn't you also have had mercy on your fellow servant, even as I had mercy on you?' His lord was angry, and delivered him to the tormentors, until he should pay all that was due to him. So my heavenly Father will also do to you, if you don't each forgive your brother truly from all his misdeeds." Matthew 18:21-35

Unforgiveness is like a cancer. It eats away at every healthy fiber of your being until you are consumed. Having unforgiveness in your life is like having an untreated termite infestation in your house. Eventually, that infestation will take over and completely destroy your home. Unforgiveness is unforgiveness, and it's toxic.

Who do you need to forgive today—for a big offense that has stuck with you for 20 years, or a small infraction that just happened this morning?

God calls you to forgive. And when you take a moment to reflect on what Jesus did for all of us at the cross so that we can be forgiven, it helps your heart soften toward forgiveness. Not toward the offense, but toward the offender. The longer you hold onto that offense, the longer YOU stay in bondage.

God is not going to take over and heal and avenge you while you are still trying to take vengeance. You may say, "I'm not taking vengeance, I'm just mad as hell."

Jesus said in Matthew 5:28: "But I say, anyone who even looks at a woman with lust has already committed adultery with her in his heart."

The same holds true for vengeance—it's murder, even if only in our own mind. Jesus says we are not to make room for this in our thoughts. So what are you still doing holding onto past offenses when you are looking to build something beautiful?

Say your old home had a faulty floorboard that caused you to trip and fall and end up in the hospital for days and out of work for weeks, with a scar for life. Now imagine you're in your new home: Would you continue to think about, revisit, seek revenge against and refuse to move on from the old one? No, of course not. You wouldn't give that stupid floorboard a second thought, nor would you treat a new floorboard in your new house any differently because of what was wrong with the old.

Whatever you are holding on to, let it go!

❤ A WILLING HEART

God knows we are not perfect. Perfection is not what He is

looking for. God is looking for willingness. Psalm 51:17 says it best: "My sacrifice, O God, is a broken spirit; a broken and contrite heart you, God, will not despise."

When we come to Him with a willing heart, we say, "God, I messed up on my own. I need you. If you don't step in, I will be sure to mess it up again."

God is asking for our willingness to let God be God.

The challenging part for us is when God doesn't do things the way we expect Him to. Perhaps He doesn't avenge us the way we hoped He would, or give us what we wanted. And often times His timing differs from ours. Please remember that we are not God. We can't see the big picture, but He can. It isn't always about us.

It's like those reality television shows that document the building of a new house. For some reason during the process, they usually allow the homeowners to come in and check out the work. I always ask myself, WHY?

The homeowners don't have a clue as to what goes into building a house, nor do they understand the reasons for building delays. So why are they there? I know builders are notorious for spending more and taking longer than expected, so we tend not to trust them. But we can trust our Builder. Let God do His work, just give Him your willing heart.

♥ FAITH

Hebrews 11:6 says: "For without faith it is impossible to please God."

What is faith?

Let's look at Hebrews 11:1: "Now faith is the substance of things hoped for, the evidence of things not seen."

Many of us confuse faith with hope. But it's not—it's the evidence of things not seen! So as you journey down this new path of right thinking, there are going to be countless times where you need to step out in faith. You will need faith to say something different than you have in the past. You will need faith to respond in a way fitting of where you want to go, not where you've been. It takes faith to be caught in the middle of two worlds—the world you are leaving behind and the one you are pressing on towards.

When those automatic thoughts and feelings come back with a vengeance—and believe me, at some stressful time, they will—you will have to exercise faith to speak God's word and your new thought pattern.

He didn't take you this far to drop you. The foundation that God builds can withstand any storm.

Elise's story exemplifies this well:

Elise was an administrative assistant for a small law firm. She was a hard worker and truly cared about the firm's clients.

However, growing up, she was met with a constant supply of criticism. Nothing was ever good enough. That spilled over into her first marriage. Elise felt like she couldn't do anything right, despite how great a wife she actually was.

At the law firm, people would nicely bring her things that needed to be corrected—since no one is perfect—and Elise would fall apart inside. She would lie awake at night, running through her mind negative thoughts they must be thinking about her. She would wonder how long until she lost her job.

During our work together, there was a common pattern in Elise's automatic thoughts and feelings: She constantly felt inferior and was waiting to be discarded.

We worked through those thoughts and feelings and found out what God had to say about her. Two scriptures helped Elise see her way through these feelings and helped her see herself through God's eyes:

> "There is neither Jew nor Greek, there is neither slave nor free, there is no male and female, for you are all one in Christ Jesus."
>
> GALATIANS 3:28
>
> "'For I know the plans I have for you,' declares the LORD, 'plans to prosper you and not to harm you, plans to give you hope and a future.'"
>
> JEREMIAH 29:11

I will admit, it did take Elise quite a bit of practice before she stopped feeling foolish and started believing what God said about her. It was then that she was able to rewrite her story. She was able to look at herself in a new light and say much more positive things about herself.

Her rewrite translated into how she carried herself. She became more assertive and sure of herself in the office, and she no longer took critiques personally or dreaded being discarded for not being perfect. Elise felt on top of the world.

Then the storm came. The law firm was dissolving, and Elise was going to be out of work. All of her old thoughts and feelings came rushing back like a flood. We worked together to build a dam to stop the flood and remember that it takes faith in times like this. God is still God. His word is still true, so therefore her new thoughts about herself were still true.

Elise held her head high and trusted. On the final day of work, one of the partners of the law firm called her into his office. Not one of the attorneys she worked closely with, she couldn't imagine what he wanted.

He wanted her to come work for him at his new office—not as his administrative assistant but as his office manager. Her pay would be almost double what it was in the old position.

She was speechless as he said that he had witnessed how she took critiques with ease and always had a positive attitude; he was impressed that nothing seemed to rattle her.

Wow! Nothing seemed to rattle her—that's the impression this woman who felt inferior and ready to be discarded gave off after she did the hard, important work.

In addition, Elise is now a leader with her church youth group. God is using her to help young girls build their self-esteem and understand who they are in Christ.

God truly does build something beautiful out of broken pieces. Every time.

*"When they had all had enough,
He said to His disciples, gather
up now the fragments, so that
nothing may be lost and wasted."*

~JOHN **6:12 (AMP)**

9
Nothing Is Wasted

Think about those television programs on HGTV that chronicle decorators styling a home (yes, I admit it, I am hooked on HGTV). I find it fascinating how they don't just go out and buy a bunch of brand new accessories; they actually personalize the home with a mix of some new and some old items.

But what I find most amazing is how they transform the old. They'll take an old door that most of us would look at as garbage and make something amazing out of it—turn it into a one-of-a-kind conversation piece. With just a little creativity, all of a sudden a piece of trash is transformed into a treasure.

That's what God does for us. He takes everything we have been through—every tear, every moan, every heartbreak, every disappointment, every evil committed against us— and uses it to make a masterpiece.

I know one of the most difficult verses to hear when you are going through a challenge is Romans 8:28: "And we know that God causes everything to work together for the good of those who love God and are called according to his purpose for them." (NLT)

WHEN YOU TRUST GOD, EVERYTHING YOU GO THROUGH WORKS OUT FOR YOUR GOOD.

It's hard to hear because when you are in the midst of a tough time, you can't fathom how what you're enduring could be good. Let me be clear: I'm not saying that the difficult time itself is good. I am saying that, if you trust Him, it works out for your good.

I have experienced this countless times in my life—God not only healed me of my brokenness, He took ALL those shattered pieces and made them into something special and unique.

Growing up, my search for love left me with a sense of worthlessness and insecurity. I would never show it on the outside, but on the inside I was sad and distraught. He now uses all of those experiences to work through me to help countless women understand their worth and value in Christ.

I spent my young life with big aspirations. Even though there were times, as a child, when I just wanted to die because I was so depressed, there was a deeper part of me that knew I was gifted and that I had purpose in this life. I took that confidence, turned it into arrogance, and headed down a loveless and self-serving road through the wilderness. I thought I had all the answers. It was a long journey with many twists and turns.

Can you imagine not only being in the wilderness and continually getting lost, but not even knowing that you're lost? I imagine this is how the Israelites felt on their 11-day journey that took 40 years.

But the wonderful thing about God is that when He has a purpose, it will be fulfilled. When you finally reach the point where you turn it all over to Him—this is a crucial role you must play, He won't "make you" fulfill your purpose—He will move heaven and earth to make it happen and make sure nothing is wasted, nothing is lost. When I came to that revelation, it was amazing.

His purpose will come to pass even if He needs to put you on warp speed to get you there. So don't think for a second that you have wasted so much of your life that you can never catch up. That's a lie from the pit of hell to keep you trapped where you are.

I am here to tell you that when God steps in He brings everything you need to be everything He has called you to be.

Often times the very thing that is causing you pain is part of your purpose. I never realized that there was a purpose in my not fitting in as a kid. I had friends, but like most young girls, my desire to be one of the cool kids was immense. They liked me, but I was not a regular part of the club.

Little did I know back then that God created that feeling of being an outsider for a reason: When you don't fit in, or aren't accepted, it is often because He is setting you apart for a greater purpose. Leaders often have to stand alone.

He will even use the evil people of this world to advance you. Yes, the people who you consider to be a thorn in your side or those oppressing you or speaking evil against you—He will use them to your advantage. I have seen this countless times in the lives of my clients, and in my own life.

I have known for a long time that my life's purpose is to help people heal their brokenness and become all they were created to be. Having lived so much of my life so far from my purpose, I know the effects that brokenness can have on driving emotions and decisions. I see this in my own blended family now. I see the effects of brokenness from a divorce. I see the effects of brokenness that comes when parents are not following God in their lives, and it breaks my heart. It's like a dam with a breach: You try to plug up the leak, but another sprouts up at the other end; and just when you get to the newest leak, two more holes form. Eventually, the dam breaks completely and the resulting flood damages everything in sight.

This is what I see constantly in families, especially blended families and particularly in my own blended family. But instead of getting bitter about the wickedness of a faulty court system, God has taken this thorn in my side and actually turned it into a tool to help others in similar situations. As a blended family counselor, I can speak not only from book knowledge, but also from firsthand experience of the damage that an angry, vengeful ex-spouse can do to children. I now get to speak to these innocent souls in hopes of repairing their brokenness before more destruction is created. I get to see the brokenness in an ex-spouse that never got healed and the damaging effects it has on so many others, and it drives me to want to help those who are willing to want more out of life.

If that is not an example of God using my enemy for my good, I don't what is.

Lily had a similar story. Lily had trust issues, but not with other people—she didn't trust her own instincts. She grew up in an alcoholic home. It wasn't the typical experience you might think of, though. Her father wasn't an angry, scene-making drunk. Quite the contrary, she could always count on him. But his life did revolve around drinking—he had a drink every night to relax from the day. He also drank a lot at parties—and they always had parties. Whatever the occasion, there was a reason to drink.

Lily grew up with her truster broken. She felt something was wrong with her father, the man she depended upon, but he always had such great reasons for drinking, and he didn't act like a drunk. So, Lily thought maybe it was just her imagination that he had a problem. And her mom never complained; in fact, she just ran around all day catering to everyone.

But something was off. There was no substance to any of the relationships in the family, because substance abuse drove everything. Lily later learned that her parents both had their own addictions: her dad's was alcohol and her mom's was food. No one ever dealt with anything, they just ate or drank.

After Lily left for college, she found herself falling into the same trap: She would party on the weekends and eat on the weekdays. Her weight climbed and her self-esteem plummeted.

Seeing the writing on the wall, Lily took action. She checked herself into a program to help with these addictive behaviors. During her journey, she learned much about the psychological aspect of addictions; they intrigued her so much that she changed her major in college. She is now Dr. Lily.

Dr. Lily spends her days healing others because she allowed God to use the enemy meant to harm her for her own good, and now she gives Him the glory.

You've heard the saying, "Everything happens for a reason." Often times these words are spoken to help someone feel better about a bad situation or to justify what has happened. But I'm here to challenge you today to change that saying to: "Everything with God happens for good reason."

Let Him take over. He'll take your broken pieces and make a masterpiece.

"For I am about to do something new. See, I have already begun! Do you not see it? I will make a pathway through the wilderness. I will create rivers in the dry wasteland."

~ISAIAH **43:19**

10
Keep Going During Inevitable Setbacks

When I worked in the fitness industry, I would get clients started on the way toward achieving their goals by helping them build a strong foundation, much like we've done here. In that case, the foundation we built was posture.

My personal training team and I knew that proper postural position was the key to accomplishing fitness goals. Without it, results were mediocre at best and injuries were common.

But for many clients, their posture had been so poor for so long that the new, better aligned position we guided them to felt awkward. It was different, and therefore uncomfortable. After an initial postural assessment was complete and postural distortions corrected, almost every client had the same reaction: They stood there holding the new position and said, "Do you expect me to move like this?" I would answer yes! But I would also remind them that it wouldn't be easy. They would have to give themselves constant reminders—chest up, shoulders back, head aligned with shoulders, hips neutral, feet forward, core pulled in.

It was a lot for someone who had been hunched over a keyboard for the past 15 years to remember and implement. But it was exactly what was necessary for them to create the foundation on which to build a healthier, fitter body.

The same is true for your emotional healing. At this point in your journey, you may be able to stand up straight in the privacy of your own home, but what happens when storms hit? What happens when unexpected situations challenge your thoughts and beliefs? You will need to give yourself constant reminders to keep you in your new, aligned position. Armed with the following guidelines, you won't lose your healing, no matter what pitfall happens.

The most common pitfall is **thinking that everything will be great from here.** This is a setup for depression and disaster. Life is full of challenges and disappointments. By reading this book and completing the exercises, you've done important work to squash old core beliefs and to think more in line with what God says.

But God never said our lives will be perfect. In fact, in Matthew 7:24-25, Jesus assured us that storms will come: "Anyone who listens to my teaching and follows it is wise, like a person who builds a house on solid rock. Though the rain comes in torrents and the floodwaters rise and the winds beat against that house, it won't collapse because it is built on bedrock."

Even with this encouragement, setbacks can still feel devastating, as they did to my client, Cynthia. One day, Cynthia came to my office, flopped herself down on the couch and whispered these words: "I think you're going to have to fix me all over again."

First, I smiled softly to myself. Cynthia was a perfectionist. If everything wasn't perfect, she bounced between feeling depressed and irate. When we worked through her core beliefs, we discovered that she felt approval came from her performance. After working through her automatic thoughts and discovering what God expected of her, she was so pleased to embrace how imperfect she was. But just that week she experienced stress at the office and reacted in a way that hurt others. She was very disappointed in herself. "After everything that I have worked through, I shouldn't have reacted like that. I must still be a bad person."

After a few minutes of reassurance that Cynthia had indeed made tremendous progress, we worked through the new thoughts that crept in. It didn't take long for Cynthia to recognize that she was expecting to be perfect again. She forgave herself and left knowing what she could have done better, with a plan for next time.

Another common pitfall is **not taking the time to determine where an attack is coming from.** Storms will come, this we know, but there are different storms in life. Some are the result of our actions—these are consequences. Others are a spiritual storm, and still other storms come as a test. Being able to decipher the type of attack is an important way to keep you from slipping back into your old belief system.

When you have come to terms with your broken pieces, your brokenness no longer drives you. So the next time you find yourself faced with a challenge, ask yourself and the Holy Spirit where it is coming from. If you sowed gossip and discord and now you are reaping what you've sown, you have some repenting to do—our God is faithful to forgive all of our sins.

If the enemy is coming against you without legal right, then you have some warfare to do, sister. Tell Satan to beat it in the name of Jesus and praise your Heavenly Father for all the work He is doing in your life. The enemy is not going to go away just because you've experienced some healing and breakthrough, but rest assured, if he is trying to attack you, you must be a force to be reckoned with. Don't back up, don't back down.

Challenges arise when you **neglect your physical needs.** I can't begin to tell you the number of my clients who, suffering from one issue or another, don't sleep enough, drink enough water, or eat right—which only makes the issue worse. You need to do what you need to do to take care of the temple God has given you. If you don't take good care of your car—regular oil changes and the like— it will breakdown and have problems with much more frequency. The same is true for your body.

Another pitfall is **not having a support system in place.** It's known that a great number of prisoners released into society wind up back in jail when they don't set up support systems to help them through their new stage of life. Similarly, you need a support system for your healing and your new phase of life. For example, a woman who has been battling against codependent behaviors and low self-esteem needs a system outside of those she regularly interacts with, chiefly her verbally abusive husband and overbearing, guilt-producing in-laws. Without such a system, it would be very difficult for her to stay in healing.

A counselor is a great place to start, but also having family and friends to aid in this endeavor will greatly contribute to your success.

The last common pitfall that occurs when storms come is **getting stuck,** as Susan did.

When Susan came to see me, she was frozen. She had come so far. She had made her way out of many needy reactions that she had once been so comfortable with. But now, she felt stuck. Faced with a rejection she wasn't expecting, Susan knew what she needed to do, but couldn't seem to move, act or respond. Instead, she retreated from life, ignoring all attempts by friends and family to help her through.

Getting stuck is not uncommon, and it happens at times of your life when you least expect it, when you feel you are doing great. It helps to understand some common reasons for becoming stuck:

- The first is self-pity. Self-pity will keep you stuck better than a river of quicksand. It pulls you under with its self-defeating mannerisms and blinds you to the truth and the reality of your situation.
- The other is taking things personally. People are not perfect. If you take personally what others do, you will

spend way too much time being hurt and reacting out of old thought patterns. You can never truly know why other people do or say what they do or say. But you have a choice not to take it to heart. Think of Proverbs 4:23: "Guard your heart above all else, for it determines the course of your life."

In order to avoid the common pitfalls, you must keep moving. Do you want to be a stagnant pond or a living stream?

"Regardless of your lot in life, you can build something beautiful on it."

~ZIG ZIGLAR

11

Are You Ready for Something Beautiful?

I spent my life pursuing things. Whether it was love, a big home or success, I was always on a mission. But I had it backwards. In pursuing the trappings of life, I was trying to add the decorative finishes to my home before it was fully built.

It wasn't until I read Matthew 6:33 and it hit me like a ton of bricks. Here's how it reads in the amplified version of the Bible:

"But seek first of all His kingdom and His righteousness [His way of doing and being right], and then all these things taken together will be given you besides."

I spent all of my time pursuing what I wanted, when all God wanted me to do was to pursue HIM. I didn't have to worry one bit about any of my needs or desires, because He had them waiting for me.

Our God is an interior decorator who comes in when you least expect it with all of the beautiful pieces that will transform your home into something truly unique. You are responsible only for building a strong foundation, sturdy walls and a solid roof—God comes in and decorates for you, at no charge!

After he's finished, when you walk into your space, you won't believe your eyes. Never in a million years would you have been able to produce anything that would even come close to what He has done.

WHEN GOD STEPS IN AND PUTS ON THE FINISHING TOUCHES, WE ARE LEFT SPEECHLESS.

I'm reminded again of those home makeover shows and the final unveiling of the redesign to the homeowners. Their expressions are always priceless: Some cry, some scream, others squeal in excitement. But I have never seen anyone say, "Eh, it's OK." Quite the contrary, they are blown away at how everything came together and appears so much more spectacular than they could have imagined.

You don't see these homeowners going over and lifting the flooring or checking behind the walls; they trust that the structure is sound and they are able to bask in the blessing that is their new home.

That's how God works. When He steps in and puts on the finishing touches, we are left speechless.

Tears come to my eyes when I see how everything I have been through has been recreated in all of the decorative pieces of my life. I remember the first few months of my walk with God, which were on warp speed. I couldn't get enough of HIM. And my life changed: He pulled me out of situations that I had been trapped in for years, I received a 60 percent pay increase in my job, I broke free from a destructive relationship, I moved into a bigger home and I finally knew what happiness felt like. This was in the first months, and all I did was seek Him.

My life has been a continuous example of Matthew 6:33: When I pursued "things" I fell short and got frustrated. When I pursued Him, he took care of everything. He changed my family, and He blessed me with a beautiful home, a secure future and peace!

Your peace and blessings are waiting for you. All of the "things" that we pursue—happiness, relationships, jobs, good health, peace, joy—can all be attained just by seeking Him. They just fall into your lap when you're not looking. That's the key—when you're not looking. Because when you're looking at achieving all the stuff, you're not seeking Him.

Our God is greater than any home makeover show. He is the designer that never leaves. God will continually beautify His daughters.

❤ THE WAY FROM HERE

I know at this point in your life you may only be conscious of the broken pieces. Hopefully after reading this book, you see those broken pieces with clarity and compassion, and now have tools to change the way you think about them so that you can make different choices for yourself. But I'm guessing that, although you're ready for the beautiful part, it still feels far away.

Hear me say this: No matter what troubles you may have experienced, joy and beauty absolutely await you. Remember, Jesus came so that we could have life and have it more abundantly (John 10:10).

Travel with me for a moment to John 16. Jesus is talking to his disciples and he is preparing them for his departure. He is assuring them suffering and persecution but he leaves them with these words:

> *"Are you asking one another what I meant when I said, 'In a little while you will see me no more, and then after a little while you will see me'? Very truly I tell you, you will weep and mourn while the world rejoices. You will grieve, but your grief will turn to joy. A woman giving birth to a child has pain because her time has come; but when her baby is born she forgets the anguish because of her joy that a child is born into the world. So with you: Now is your time of grief, but I will see you again and you will rejoice, and no one will take away your joy. In that day you will no longer ask me anything. Very truly I tell you, my Father will give you whatever you ask in my name. Until now you have not asked for anything in my name. Ask and you will receive, and your joy will be complete."*

> *"Though I have been speaking figuratively, a time is coming when I will no longer use this kind of language but will tell you plainly about my Father. In that day*

you will ask in my name. I am not saying that I will ask the Father on your behalf. No, the Father himself loves you because you have loved me and have believed that I came from God. I came from the Father and entered the world; now I am leaving the world and going back to the Father." (John 16:19-28)

"Do you now believe?" Jesus replied. "A time is coming and in fact has come when you will be scattered, each to your own home. You will leave me all alone. Yet I am not alone, for my Father is with me.

"I have told you these things, so that in me you may have peace. In this world you will have trouble. But take heart! I have overcome the world." (John 16:31-33)

What I take from these passages is this: In this world, you will have trouble. Meaning, you are not a fairy princess whose life will be perfect. But—I love that word, especially when it's followed by a promise—take heart: In your troubles, the seeds of perfection are born. Through the healing grace of our God, you will overcome the world.

When Jesus says he has overcome the world, he means he has overcome everything that opposes the plans of God. That's amazing news, because if Jesus has overcome the world, you can too.

So the next time trouble, a challenge or persecution comes your way, don't get bent out of shape. Instead, take your renewed mind and the love and grace given to you by our Lord and Savior and laugh, knowing that "My God works all things together for my good and His glory." And that you can overcome anything in this world.

Keep that attitude and you will see that God steps in and gives you a home makeover over and over and over again. You will never again have to live in brokenness.

And you too will have the opportunity to tell how God built something beautiful out of your broken pieces. ♥

NOTES

APPENDIX

Understand Your Needs
by Knowing Your Temperament

Your temperament has a lot to do with how you respond to core beliefs and the wounds that impacted you, because it plays a major role in how you relate to people, places and things.

To give you a better understanding of temperament, first think about your personality. You've encountered personality tests before, right? While they are fun to take and do tell us a little bit about ourselves (that we probably already knew), they only speak of the "outward" self.

These tests may lead you to conclude, "I'm a total introvert," or, "I'm type A." While these statements may be true, they only give you a peek, and a small one at that, into your true nature. In fact, your personality is superficial. It's the persona, or the mask, you wear to manipulate how others see you—and how you see yourself.

Your temperament dictates your "inward" self—your inner workings, the values that drive you and the innate gifts that only you have. Temperament is also the determining factor in how well you handle the pressures of life.

Knowing your temperament is like having an instruction manual for finding fulfillment in all areas of your life. There are five different basic temperaments, each of which are broken down into the following three categories:

- **The first category is Inclusion.** The need for Inclusion relates to forming new relationships and associating with others; it determines the extent of contact and prominence that a person seeks. It also measures intellectual energies.

- **The second category is Control.** The need for Control relates to decision-making, influence and persuasion between people; it determines the extent of power or dominance that a person seeks.

- **The third category is Affection.** The need for Affection relates to emotional ties and warm connections between people; it determines the extent of closeness that a person seeks.

Each category is further broken down into two subcategories—meaning that a full temperament analysis is very deep and more complex than I can cover in a short book. Yet, while it's impossible to determine your exact temperament without a full analysis, you may see yourself in one of these overviews and learn more about how you respond to brokenness.

The five basic temperaments are:

1. MELANCHOLY

In general, melancholy is the moodiest of the five temperaments. Those with melancholy temperaments are very private people who work hard to protect that privacy.

♥

In Inclusion, their social skills usually place them in a loner environment where they distance themselves from most people (except family). Their circle of friends is often quite small, but they are very close to those in their circle. They tend to battle letting their mind dwell on the negative, which typically results in a downward spiral of their thought pattern. They struggle to understand more outgoing temperament types.

For those who are eager for deep healing and better relationships, I encourage you to visit my website at www.krisreece.com and sign up to receive your free "What's My Temperament?" quiz to go further toward determining your specific temperament.

In Control, melancholy temperaments are rebels. While they desire very little control over the lives of others, they cannot tolerate anyone telling them what to do. They are self-motivated and make good leaders.

In Affection, they do not give or receive a lot of love; however, they have very deep, tender feelings. They would do anything for their family and loved ones.

In a wounded situation, melancholy temperaments relate to their wounds in a negative, self-defeating manner. Sad to say, but those who are melancholy are most likely to commit suicide. This is due in part to their negative thinking. When melancholy temperaments learn to control their thinking, they tend to move well through the healing process, especially if they are surrounded by people they love and trust.

2. PHLEGMATIC

In general, this is the most laid back of all the temperaments. Phlegmatics tend to long for peace and will avoid confrontation. They are also the only temperament that can truly blend with others, creating a more calm, stable temperament in total.

In Inclusion, Phlegmatics are very positive in their approach to relationships and don't fear rejection. They are slow-paced, tire easily and tend to observe rather than participate. They also have a tremendous capacity for tasks.

In Control, those with this temperament are the negotiators or peacemakers. They are highly independent and do not like to be controlled; however, they do like to work in a team. They tend to not want to expend too much energy, making them good delegators.

In Affection, Phlegmatics don't require a great deal of love, although they give the appearance of wanting love and affection. They are stable in this area but tend to want to reserve their energy level.

In a wounded situation, those with a Plegmatic temperament will often brush off the wound and downplay its effects in an effort to not expend too much energy thinking about it. Or, they may actually have an easier time finding peace in the situation.

3. SUPINE

In general, supines are servants. Supine temperaments are so tenderhearted and gentle that, sadly, they allow many people to use them.

In Inclusion, Supines are difficult to read. They appear to be introverts when they are actually extroverts. They want to be included but rarely make the initiative. Rather, they leave it up to others, and when others don't reach out, Supines feel rejected. They expect others to read their mind while showing no outward signs that they are interested in socializing.

In Control, those with this temperament don't like to make decisions alone. They like others to be involved in the process, and often they will let others control them while internalizing anger about being controlled. They are very loyal and enjoy serving those they love.

In Affection, this temperament has a DEEP need for love and may go into a depression without it. When they feel safe in a relationship, they can open up, but they often have a problem initiating love and expect others to read what it is they want. Because of this, they are the temperament most easily hurt by others.

In a wounded situation, Supines suffer from a victim mentality, and because of their need to be loved, they are always looking to someone else. If their wounds are not healed, they tend to trust the wrong people and continually get hurt.

4. SANGUINE

In general, this is the most talkative of all the temperaments. Sanguines are impulsive and can be moody.

In Inclusion, those with this temperament are very social and talkative. They are friendly and extroverted. They are not task-oriented and must be around people or they become stressed. Sanguines tend to dominate a conversation and even exaggerate at times. This can bother some of the other temperaments, especially Melancholy.

In Control, Sanguines are rare, but in such cases they have an upbeat attitude, can be aggressive and are responsible. When they approach burnout, they tend to swing in the opposite direction and want others to take control. This often happens without notice and can confuse people.

In Affection, those with this temperament are the most lovable, both in the amount they give and the amount they require. They like to touch and hug to show affection. They must be told daily that they are loved, and they tend to feel devastated when they are not, which can drain some other temperaments. With Sanguines in Affection, it never seems like they are getting enough love.

In a wounded situation, Sanguines try hard to get their

needs met. When they are unsuccessful, they are able to move on with the belief that the next relationship will meet their needs. They have trouble facing their problems because they have trouble focusing in general. They also struggle with controlling their anger and discipline.

5. CHOLERIC

In general, those with a Choleric temperament make things happen. A Choleric who has let God be in control is task-oriented, strong-minded, confident and caring. The Choleric who doesn't allow God to rule their world can be dominating mean, cruel and downright nasty and controlling.

In Inclusion, Cholerics are task-oriented and focused more on their accomplishments than relationships. If they do not receive recognition for their accomplishments, they become angry. They are very fast-paced and can take on a variety of tasks and work until they burn out.

In Control, those with this temperament are independent and capable of making decisions and taking on a tremendous amount of responsibility. They will not, however, be controlled by others. They make great leaders if they let God lead them. Most other temperaments do not like the efficient, military-like approach of Cholerics.

In Affection, Cholerics will only have a few deep relationships, which must be on their terms. They struggle with loving people for who they are and rather look to people for what they can do for them.

In a wounded situation, Cholerics are the least likely to reach out for help. In fact, they are the least likely to think they have a problem, and typically think the problem belongs to the partner in their relationship. In many cases, the people in relationships with Cholerics are the ones that come to see me for counseling.

I could spend an entire book delving in to the intricacies of each of the temperaments in each of the categories. And that wouldn't even begin to cover how to navigate the many ways your temperament interacts with the temperaments of your partner, kids, friends and family members. But when you have this information, it's like a roadmap to relationships—very powerful indeed.

To take another step toward understanding your own needs—and the needs of you're the people in your life— visit *www.krisreece.com/beautiful-life-book* and download your copy of the "What's My Temperament?" quiz.

Scripture Remedies for Common Negative Feelings and Thoughts

You have the power to overcome any negative thought patterns and feelings by replacing them with the Word of God. In doing so, since the Word of God is the truth, rather than simply telling the thoughts and feelings to go away, you are supplanting them with more productive and accurate ideas.

As soon as one of the thoughts or feelings listed below pops into your heart and mind, read and reflect on the corresponding Scripture—and to take it one step further, use the Blank Journal Page on page XX of this appendix to come up with and record a new thought.

The Scripture quoted below comes from the Amplified Bible unless otherwise noted; I enjoy the way it expands God's word.

You may also download and print a copy of this resource from my website, *krisreece.com/beautiful-life-book*, so that you can keep multiple copies handy for reference whenever old beliefs pop up.

Abandonment

"He Himself has said, I will not in any way fail you nor give you up nor leave you without support. [I will] not, [I will] not, [I will] not in any degree leave you helpless nor forsake nor let [you] down! [Assuredly not!]" ~HEBREWS 13:5

Anger

"Let all bitterness and indignation and wrath [passion, rage, bad temper] and resentment [anger, animosity] and quarreling [brawling, clamor, contention] and slander [evil-speaking, abusive or blasphemous language] be banished from you, with all malice [spite, ill will, or baseness of any kind]. And become useful and helpful and kind to one another, tenderhearted [compassionate, understanding, loving-hearted], forgiving one another [readily and freely], as God in Christ forgave you." ~EPHESIANS 4:31-32

"I will be quick to hear [a ready listener], slow to speak, slow to take offense and to get angry. For my anger does not promote the righteousness God [wishes and requires]." ~JAMES 1:19-20

Anxiety and worry

"I will not worry or be anxious about tomorrow, for tomorrow will have worries and anxieties of its own. Sufficient for each day is its own trouble." ~MATTHEW 6:34

"My worrying and being anxious will not add one unit of measure [cubit] to my stature or to the span of my life." ~MATTHEW 6:27

Dirty

"I will [freely] admit that I have sinned and confess my sins, He is faithful and just [true to His own nature and promises] and will forgive my sins [dismiss our lawlessness] and [continuously] cleanse me from all unrighteousness [everything not in conformity to His will in purpose, thought, and action]." ~JOHN 1:9

Distrust

"When I am afraid, I will have confidence in and put my trust and reliance in You. By [the help of] God I will praise His word; on God I lean, rely, and confidently put my trust; I will not fear. What can man, who is flesh, do to me?" ~PSALM 56:3-4

"The fear of man brings a snare, but whoever leans on, trusts in, and puts his confidence in the Lord is safe and set on high." ~PROVERBS 29:25

Doubt

"I will be in faith that He asks with no wavering [no hesitating, no doubting]. For the one who wavers [hesitates, doubts] is like the billowing surge out at sea that is blown hither and thither and tossed by the wind." ~JAMES 1:6

Fear

"God will cover me with His pinions, and under His wings I will trust and find refuge; His truth and His faithfulness are a shield and a buckler. I shall not be afraid of the terror of the night, nor of the arrow [the evil plots and slanders of the wicked] that flies by day." ~PSALM 91:4-5

Guilt

"Because Christ lives in me [then, although] my [natural] body is dead by reason of sin and guilt, the spirit is alive because of [the] righteousness [that He imputes to me]." ~ROMANS 8:10

"God does not condemn me because He has justified me, Jesus does not condemn me because He is seated at the right hand of God and is interceding for me." ~ROMANS 8:33-34

Hopelessness

"I will say to myself, 'The Lord is my inheritance; therefore, I will hope in him!' The Lord is good to those who depend on him, to those who search for him. So it is good to wait quietly for help from the Lord." ~LAMENTATIONS 3:24-26

"The Lord has His eye upon those who fear Him [who revere and worship Him with awe], who wait for Him and hope in His mercy and loving-kindness." ~PSALM 33:18

Insecurity

"I will fear not, for God is with me; I am not dismayed; for He is my God. He will strengthen me, yes, He will help me, He will uphold me with His righteous right hand." ~ISAIAH 41:10

"No weapon formed against me shall prosper, and every tongue that rises against me in judgment I shall show to the in the wrong. This [peace, righteousness, security, triumph over opposition] is my inheritance because I am a servant of the Lord." ~Isaiah 54:17

Laziness

"I know your [record of] works and what you are doing; you are neither cold nor hot. Would that you were cold or hot! So, because you are lukewarm and neither cold nor hot, I will spew you out of my mouth!" ~Revelation 3:15-16

"Better is he who is lightly esteemed but works for his own support than he who assumes honor for himself and lacks bread." ~Proverbs 12:9

Out of Control

"The love of Christ controls me." ~2 Corinthians 5:14

"I am a God-pleaser, not a people-pleaser. I obey God before man." ~Acts 5:29

Powerlessness

"He gives power to the faint and weary, and to him who has no might He increases strength [causing it to multiply and making it abound]." ~Isaiah 40:29

"I have been given authority and power over all the power that the enemy [possesses]; and nothing shall in any way harm me." ~Luke 10:19

Pride

"When swelling and pride come, then emptiness and shame come also, but with the humble [those who are lowly, who have been pruned or chiseled by trial, and renounce self] are skillful and godly Wisdom and soundness." ~PROVERBS 11:2

"Pride lands me flat on my face, but humility prepares me for honor." ~PROVERBS 29:23 [THE MESSAGE]

Rejection

"If God is for me, who can be against me?" ~ROMANS 8:31

"When I go someplace and the people don't receive and accept me, I don't let it get me down, I just shake it off and go on about my business." ~LUKE 10:10-11

Unlovableness

"For God so greatly loved and dearly prized the world that He [even] gave up His only begotten [unique] Son, so that whoever believes in [trusts in, clings to, relies on] Him shall not perish [come to destruction, be lost] but have eternal [everlasting] life." ~JOHN 3:16

"God loves those who love Him, and those who seek Him early and diligently shall find Him." ~PROVERBS 8:17

Unforgiveness

"If I forgive people their trespasses [their reckless and willful sins, leaving them, letting them go, and giving up resentment], my heavenly Father will also forgive me." ~MATTHEW 6:14

"And whenever I stand praying, if I have anything against anyone, I forgive him and let it drop [leave it, let it go], in order that my Father who is in heaven may also forgive me my [own] failings and shortcomings and let them drop. But if I do not forgive, neither will my Father in heaven forgive my failings and shortcomings." ~MARK 11:25-26

Victimization

"Yet amid all these things we are more than conquerors and gain a surpassing victory through Him Who loved us." ~ROMANS 8:37

Worthlessness

"And in accordance with this will [of God], I have been made holy [consecrated and sanctified] through the offering made once for all of the body of Jesus Christ [the Anointed One]." ~HEBREWS 10:10

"For I know the thoughts and plans that I have for you, says the Lord, thoughts and plans for welfare and peace and not for evil, to give you hope in your final outcome." ~JEREMIAH 29:11

Blank Journal Page

Here is a blank journal page you can use to complete the assignment from Chapter 7: God Is the Master Builder.

There is also a digital version of this page on my website, at *www.krisreece.com/beautiful-life-book,* that you can print out and use again and again.

♥ *Journal*
GOD IS THE MASTER BUILDER

♥ Situation

_____

_____

_____

_____

_____

_____

♥ Thoughts

_____

_____

_____

_____

_____

_____

♥ **Feelings**

_____
_____
_____
_____
_____
_____

♥ **God's Word**

_____
_____
_____
_____
_____
_____

♥ **New Thought**

_____
_____
_____
_____
_____
_____

ABOUT THE AUTHOR

KRIS REECE is passionate about helping people break free from the chains that bind them and create an abundant life in Jesus.

No stranger to living outside the will of God, Kris spent half her life making wrong relationship choices and settling for less than best. After a tumultuous divorce, she completely surrendered to Him. Today, she knows firsthand how the seemingly broken pieces of a life can be rearranged into something beautiful.

Kris's career path began in the field of fitness, as the owner of a personal training studio. While she had fun helping people achieve physical health, she felt something was missing in her approach to creating wellness, something vital: internal healing. This longing to truly help people change from the inside out led to a complete life and career transformation.

Now, Kris spends her days counseling, coaching and speaking to women about healing their brokenness and becoming all they were created to be. She is a licensed counselor, certified life coach and certified divorce coach, and she holds an MA in Christian counseling. She is also currently working toward her PhD in Christian counseling and BA in theology.

Kris has a private practice in Warren, NJ, and lives in Hillsborough, NJ, with her husband, Jean Paul. They are the proud parents of three children—Zoe, Amanda and Zachary—and three fur babies—Daisy, Parker and Buster.

WHAT'S NEXT?

Continue the journey to your beautiful life! Visit Kris's website for many additional resources, including:

- ✓ "What's My Temperament?" quiz
- ✓ "How Broken Am I?" quiz
- ✓ Printable journal pages
- ✓ Printable list of "Scriptures to Replace Faulty Thinking"
- ✓ "How to Tell if You're in Love With a Broken Person" article

www.krisreece.com/beautiful-life-book

To ask a Kris a question or schedule a time to discuss counseling or coaching, email **kris@krisreece.com**

www.facebook.com/kris.reece.counselor.coach

THANK YOU!

Made in United States
Cleveland, OH
05 December 2024

11310855R00090